The Relational BOOK for Parenting

Saliha Bava, PhD and Mark Greene

Foreword by Kenneth J. Gergen, PhD

This book is not intended as a substitute for advice from a trained professional.

Published by Think Play Partners • ThinkPlayPartners.com • New York City
First Edition
ISBN: 978-1979378659
All Contents © 2018 by Saliha Bava and Mark Greene

Table of contents

Foreword

The new world of relational parenting

The history of child rearing research is a product of Western individualism. Likewise, the teeming number of manuals on how to raise children fill the bookstore shelves. All are premised on the idea of individual agents — an adult and a child — acting on each other. More specifically, it is the parent who acts on the child — loving, teaching, correcting, supporting the child's development, and so on. The child is shaped by the parent, as it is supposed. One common outcome of good child rearing is the child's autonomy. The mature person, it is reasoned, is an independent agent. How limited this view is, and how detrimental to human well-being.

That we fashion our children misses, for one, the many ways in which we as parents are shaped as well. We become different persons in the very act of relating to our children. We learn and we grow just as they do. It also misses the profound ways in which we are immersed within relationship, even when alone. What we think about, how we feel, what we choose, and indeed the very meaning we attach to life are born and draw their breath from relationship. Autonomy is a myth.

The presumption that we are separate and autonomous individuals also enters into social life. It fosters self-centeredness and justifies the exploitation of others. Self-esteem becomes a pivotal issue in everyday life. We foster a general disregard for relationships, and along with this, pleas to sacrifice for the common good.

Within the present work by my good friends Saliha Bava and Mark Greene, we enter a new and more promising world. They move beyond the traditional assumption of isolated individuals to focus on what we create together. They invite us to look beyond the single individuals to the space between, aptly called relational spaces.

They sensitize us to the ways in which our conversations create realities, and thus the vital importance of the language we use, and the stories through which we understand ourselves. They illuminate ways in which we can contribute to the well-being of the relational space — listening with curiosity, holding uncertainty, and staying playful, among them.

I will long treasure their line, "How we relate creates who we are becoming." And within this line, one can also begin to see implications of profound proportion. More generally, the traditional view of persons as independent agents is at the heart of individualist ideology. As we begin exploring the "superpowers" emerging from a relational orientation to life, so do we loosen the grip of individualism.

Thus, in small ways — relating with our children, partners, neighbors, and colleagues — we begin to transform our culture. How we relate, creates what the culture becomes. So, it is with keen appreciation that we can welcome this book into our many relationships.

Kenneth J. Gergen, PhD
Author of *Relational Being: Beyond Self and Community*

We are born out of relationships into relationships.

Saliha Bava

Pull a thread here and you'll find it's attached to the rest of the world.

Nadeem Aslam

Introduction

We're glad you're here

Conversations and relationships go hand in hand. In fact, one does not exist without the other. It is in the verbal and the non-verbal of communication that we come to exist. In our utterances and gestures, as witnessed and responded to by others, we are.

This relational call and response is the driving force of parenting. Our kids call out, and we respond. How we respond to them, in turn, shapes their next interaction with us. Who we are, and who we are becoming, emerges from this interaction and communication. As we are shaping them, they are shaping us. Through our mutual participation, we create the messy, joyous process of parenting and being raised. All of life and living, all creativity, all play, all relationships emerge from the constant back and forth of relating.

Relational thinking asks us to hold uncertainty, notice emergence and stay playful. It asks us to explore how, through the back and forth of relating, we co-create our roles as partners, parents and co-workers, how we are continually re-creating who we are, and how we make meaning.

The Relational Book for Parenting explores discourses from sociology, anthropology, physiology, psychology, philosophy, and more. It is a glorious mash-up of ideas; a window into the ongoing debate about how human beings make meaning. These sometimes competing discourses are the fuel for the conversations we want to spark, but our goal is to focus on a much more fundamental consideration: namely, what happens when we mindfully center and care for our relationships.

An important part of growing our relational intelligence is learning to engage these kinds of divergent conversations, creating space for our differences while we learn how to bridge and coordinate with them. It is in coordinating difference that we open the door to innovative new solutions.

> When we bridge and coordinate across our differences we create a more resilient web of relationships within the families and communities that are central to our collective well-being.

Unfortunately, our culture has become increasingly argumentative and reactive. Our most divisive social challenges are compounded by ideological silos and aggrivated by epidemic levels of social isolation. Research by AARP tells us that 42 million of us are "chronically lonely." If we are to heal our disconnection, we must re-focus on how to create joyful, lasting relationships. It is in relationship with each other that our collective sense of well-being resides. It is in interdependence that our more powerful human attributes are activated.

As parents, we are being called to raise the next generation, to raise the makers of our culture, to raise the leaders of tomorrow, to raise the citizens of the world. We are not only raising our children, we are raising the next generation of human beings who will respond to the call of the complex world we leave them with. We are not just raising our own children, we're raising human beings who are responsible for knitting the fabric of the world, alongside millions of others. *How will we prepare them for this?*

A simple Google search of "preparing the next generation" yields results across sectors ranging from education to entrepreneurship, from leadership to human resources, from workforce to politics. All are calling for a new set of capacities for the next generation of thinkers and entrepreneurs; the creators and innovators of tomorrow. What are these capacities? Most of them are commonly identified as:
Learning how to learn
Learning how to think (not just what to think)
Learning how to make
Learning to be flexible and collaborative problem solvers

All of these capacities are rooted in what we call relational intelligence.

By learning to listen with curiosity and ask questions, we acquire the art of being fully in conversation with others, learning how to learn.

By activating the capacity to stay playful (not only as children, but into adulthood), we gain the confidence to reconfigure, improvise, adapt, and be agile in a complex changing world.

By learning to frame and reframe our stories, we learn the art of how to make meaning, create value, and how to shape what's coming next.

By learning to track context, we come to understand how we are influenced by our cultures, histories, and circumstances both past and present. We learn how we are culture makers and thus, how we can shift and reshape context on a grand scale.

And last but not least, in becoming makers and co-creators, we don't just learn to manage uncertainty, we learn to intentionally embrace it as a powerful collaborative tool and a generative force.

The presence of our children defines us as parents, but it is the call and response of our relationship that breathes life into that role. When we make the conscious choice to grow our children's relational intelligence, we grow our own capacities as well. It cannot be otherwise. We grow these capacities not just in our role as parents, but as partners, co-workers, children in our own right, and as human beings.

As you turn the pages of our book, we hope you see play. We hope you see the joy of relating. The ideas, theories, games and stories in this book are designed to give each family entry points into relational ways of communicating, playing, and connecting. We hope these ideas will spark your family's own distinctive conversations; conversations that get richer over time, creating the kind of heartfelt connections we all long for.

Welcome to the conversation. We're glad you're here.

When we seek for connection, we restore the world to wholeness.

Margaret J. Wheatley

MARK GREENE

Welcome to the Relational Book for Parenting!

HOW WELL OUR CHILDREN ARE ABLE TO FORM *HEALTHY, AUTHENTIC RELATIONSHIPS* WILL DETERMINE THEIR SUCCESS IN BOTH THEIR *PERSONAL* AND *PROFESSIONAL* LIVES.

THIS HOLDS TRUE FOR US AS MUCH AS FOR OUR CHILDREN.

Here's the deal about our book:

THIS BOOK IS PACKED FULL OF IDEAS ABOUT HOW TO HELP KIDS (AND ADULTS) GROW *JOYFUL, CREATIVE RELATIONSHIPS.*

BECAUSE FAMILIES CAN BE WONDERFULLY DIFFERENT IN SO MANY WAYS — CROSS-CULTURAL, LGBTQ, CO-PARENTED AND MORE — WE ENCOURAGE READERS TO <u>STAY PLAYFUL</u>, TO EXPERIMENT WITH AND MODIFY THESE IDEAS IN WAYS *THAT FIT BEST FOR YOU AND YOUR FAMILY.*

SALIHA BAVA

The quality of our relationships determines the quality of our lives.

Esther Perel

Part one:
"So, here's a weird question"

OR *OUR HEARTS?* A LOT OF PEOPLE THINK OUR *FEELINGS* COME FROM OUR HEARTS.

Part two:

Relationships are key

A BIG PART OF CREATING FULFILLING PERSONAL AND PROFESSIONAL LIVES COMES DOWN TO HOW WELL WE FORM *HEALTHY, JOYFUL RELATIONSHIPS.*

Our children's relationships include:

- *Family relationships*
- *Friendships*
- *Relationships with teachers, coaches, and others*

As they become adults...

- *Business relationships*
- *Romantic relationships*
- *Relationships with their larger community*

> WE CALL THE CAPACITY TO CREATE AND CARE FOR RELATIONSHIPS **"RELATIONAL INTELLIGENCE"** (MANY OTHERS USE THIS TERM, TOO.)

When our children grow their relational intelligence, they are better able to

- self-regulate emotionally
- resist negative peer pressure
- engage others' points of view
- form authentic relationships
- grow self-confidence
- value difference
- collaborate and co-create
- relate in caring ways

Caring relationships are the building blocks for creating robust, healthy societies.

 MUCH LIKE LEARNING TO SPEAK A NEW LANGUAGE, GROWING OUR CHILDREN'S (AND OUR OWN) RELATIONAL INTELLIGENCE IS A **_TRIAL AND ERROR PROCESS._**

THIS PROCESS IS ONGOING. <u>IT CONTINUES TO TAKE PLACE OVER THE COURSE OF OUR LIFETIMES IN RELATIONSHIP WITH OTHERS.</u>

IT IS IN THE PROCESS OF EXPLORING AND ENGAGING OUR RELATIONAL CAPACITIES THAT THEY GROW.

Part three:

Remaking culture

It's up to us to give our children a different message

In researching her book *When Boys Become Boys*, Dr. Judy Chu of Stanford University was engaged as a participant observer in a classroom of four- and five-year-old children for two years.

What Chu observed was that our sons are taught to hide their early capacity for being emotionally perceptive, articulate, and responsive. Starting in preschool, they learn to align their behaviors with "the emotionally disconnected stereotype our culture projects onto them."

"Boys are taught to hide vulnerable emotions like sadness, fear, and pain, which imply weakness and are stereotypically associated with femininity," Chu states.

As they grow older, our sons are forced to "man up" in increasingly aggressive and belligerent ways. They are taught by their peers, their coaches, their teachers and even their families that real men don't share their emotions and feelings. And so, they cease exploring the nuances of relating. They hide from connection. The result is that they live isolated lives, shut off from the authentic relationships that relational capacities create.

It's no better for girls. We have a myth in our culture that says girls are free to express and connect. They are not. We limit girls and women to what might be called the greeting card school of emotional expression. We allow the expression of sympathy or celebration, but not the sharing of more complex, volatile or dark emotions. There are no greeting cards for rage or despair. These feelings our daughters are trained to hide away and suppress.

Additionally, we can unintentionally limit our children's exploration of their relational capacities. We block their relational growth by telling them the "right" ways to feel instead of helping them work through the more complex feelings that can arise for them. We might tend to correct them for getting upset, expressing emotions that make us uncomfortable; emotions like anger, sadness or fear.

Whenever we limit our children's emotional expression we cut them off from the opportunity to learn more nuanced forms of expression. Additionally, we are suppressing their capacity to form relationships. It is in relational spaces that emotions get co-created. In order to avoid unwelcome forms of expression, many children engage in more perfunctory superficial relationships, or simply withdraw from relating altogether. This withdrawal represents a pivotal moment in our children's development, because how we relate creates who we are becoming.

Our robust networks of personal and professional relationships are the source of resiliency for us during times of personal crisis, natural disasters or economic upheaval. Without a network of meaningful, joyful relationships, we are far more likely to fall into depression, isolation and chronic illness. Growing our children's relational intelligence will improve their emotional and physical health over the course of their lifetimes. In fact, it will improve every metric by which we measure quality of life.

Our culture is giving our sons a message to shut up; to not talk about what they are feeling. Our culture is telling our daughters to only express a limited set of "approved" emotions; the greeting card school of emotional expression. Without a loving and consistent counter message, our childrens' vibrant relational capacities will slowly be hidden away and silenced.

> The good news is our children are born ready to explore and grow their relationship superpowers.

Our children simply need places in which they are encouraged to grow their connections in the world instead of suppressing them. They don't need relational encouragement to be happening for them in every aspect of their lives, they simply need it to be happening in some central part.

There is no better place for this than within our own families. And when we provide our children the opportunity to grow their relational intelligence, *we help shift our culture from one of isolation to one of connection.*

Neuroscience and all sorts of evolutionary anthropology confirm that we are born naturally relational human beings ...

Our problem is we live in a culture that defines not only manhood but also maturity in ways that actually disconnect us from our relationships.

It's actually a culture clashing with nature.

Niobe Way

With our stories, and in our interactions with others, we craft our world.

Sheila McNamee

Part four:

How do we talk about talking?

SALIHA, I'M A LITTLE CONCERNED ABOUT BILLY'S SOCCER PRACTICE TODAY.
uncertainty?
?

WHEN MARK EXPRESSES "CONCERN," SALIHA MIGHT TRY TO GUESS THE PROBLEM BASED ON *HER STORIES ABOUT MARK,* AND FIX THE PROBLEM FOR HIM.

MAYBE MARK DOESN'T LIKE TAKING BILLY TO SOCCER BECAUSE MARK *DOESN'T LIKE SPORTS* ALL THAT MUCH. SO, I SHOULD TAKE HIM.

BUT SALIHA HAS A LOT ON HER SCHEDULE AND IT CAN **FEEL FRUSTRATING** TO HAVE TO TAKE BILLY TO SOCCER, TOO. THE FRUSTRATION SHE IS **FEELING** IS ROOTED IN **STORIES ABOUT MARK** THAT SHE AND MARK HAVE CO-CREATED OVER TIME.

I WISH MARK WOULDN'T ASSUME BILLY FEELS THE SAME WAY HE DOES ABOUT SOCCER.

ALL RIGHT, I HAVE A LOT TO DO, BUT HOW ABOUT I TAKE HIM TO SOCCER?
impatience?

THIS **_"LISTENING TO CONFIRM MY STORY OR OPINION"_** IS A VERY COMMON CHALLENGE FOR COUPLES AS WELL AS FOR **_PARENTS AND KIDS._**

INSTEAD, I CAN CHOOSE TO SET MY **_STORY_** ASIDE. I CAN SAY **_"I DON'T KNOW WHAT YOU ARE GOING TO TELL ME AND I'M CURIOUS TO HEAR WHAT IT IS."_**

IN SUPPORT OF THAT, I CAN INSTEAD CHOOSE TO **_ASK MORE QUESTIONS._**

LISTENING WITH CURIOSITY HELPS US SET ASIDE OUR ASSUMPTIONS ABOUT WHAT PEOPLE INTEND AND INSTEAD LOOK TO BE SURPRISED, TO MAKE A DISCOVERY.

WHEN WE SHIFT TO THIS MINDSET, WE ACTUALLY LISTEN DIFFERENTLY. THIS WAY OF LISTENING CAN ALSO MAKE OTHERS **FEEL TRULY HEARD.** WHICH SOMETIMES, IS ALL THEY REALLY NEED FROM US.

NOW IT'S MY TURN...

WHEN I SAID, *"WHY DO YOU DO THAT?"* I IGNORED SALIHA'S OFFER (TO TAKE BILLY TO SOCCER).

INSTEAD, *I CHOSE TO INTERPRET HER TONE AS NEGATIVE,* DECLARING *MY STORY* THAT SHE IS ALWAYS *JUMPING TO CONCLUSIONS.*

NOTICING WHEN SOMEONE MAKES AN *OFFER* AND PAUSING TO *ACKNOWLEDGE* IT CAN POSITIVELY SHIFT ENTIRE CONVERSATIONS.

IT'S IMPORTANT TO NOTE THAT *CONTEXT* AND A RANGE OF OTHER FACTORS IMPACT WHAT IS POSSIBLE *IN THE MOMENT.*

BUT WHEN I DISMISSED HER OFFER, I CHOSE TO FOCUS ON MY UNHELPFUL STORY ABOUT SALIHA, *ASSUMING HER TO BE IRRITATED* ...

... *WHICH IS IRRITATING FOR HER!*

THIS IS WHAT MAKES THE STORIES WE CARRY SO POWERFUL. *WE LITERALLY LIVE THE STORIES WE TELL* (AND SO DOES EVERYONE ELSE).

54

… Not-knowing refers to the belief that one person cannot pre-know another person or his or her situation or what is best for them.

Harlene Anderson

Part five:

Learning to listen

Witnessing and listening

Talking and listening are two sides of the same relational coin. How we listen determines the path a conversation will take. In fact, there are many contexts in which how we listen can have far more impact than what we say. When we are told, "You don't listen," it is likely a comment on *how we listen.* We can ask the people around us, "In our relationship, how do I typically listen? What do I not listen to?"

| At times, our children will express deeply challenging emotions. How will we listen?

Tears, frustration, sadness, and fear are difficult to witness, but people we love sometimes need for us to witness and hold difficult emotions for them. We can grow our capacity to witness strong emotions without collapsing into them. We can remain calm, not automatically having an equal or opposite emotional response, but it takes time to learn this capacity, especially if no one modeled it for us when we were young.

If we never learned how to hold the strong emotions of others, witnessing our child's difficult emotions can quickly become very uncomfortable for us. Instead of hanging in and staying engaged, we may fall back on our stories to decide why our child is feeling what they're feeling. So, even though we may be listening, we might be listening for details that confirm our theory about what is wrong. We may even listen in ways that seek to validate something we have already had a disagreement about. "I told you this would happen ..."

When we are focused on confirming our stories, our attention is distracted from the broader, more varied nuances of what our children (or partner) might be seeking to communicate. When we take the knowing position about what is happening, we are likely to miss signs of anything new or different that is emerging, thereby quashing new shoots of potential growth in order to verify our previously held assumptions.

When we set aside our assumptions and instead intentionally listen as a witness, we discover how meaningful it can be to others as we bear witness to the challenging emotions they are feeling. In these moments, we can hear more about the emotional journey our child or partner has embarked on. In our role as a witness, we can become a participant observer, asking questions, experiencing the moment, not trying to shift things.

When we do this, others can feel heard, getting the space and support they need to engage with their emotions. Our children can learn to play with what they are feeling, explore it. They learn how to hang in and be curious with their emotional responses. They can create new meanings and connections within the relational space. Our calmness becomes their calmness. Our exploration, theirs. Our patience, theirs.

As parents, we can show our children that they don't have to heighten their response, but instead see the beauty, the "wowness" of being human. Later in their lives, they can learn to say "Wow, what was that? That was strange what I felt. I wonder what that was?"

Listening is not passive. It is a powerfully active way of being.

Listening is a process of centering yourself in order to allow an experience to play out for you and your child. It is a capacity-building moment, in which we learn that when emotions play out in the back and forth of relating, wonderful new possibilities are created. Listening with curiosity gives our children opportunities to get acclimated to their own emotional expression, while having the calming comfort of our presence. We can confirm that we are listening by making simple statements like "I know it's a lot to think about," or we can ask simple questions like "how do you feel?"

In choosing to ask questions and stay curious, we help grow our children's relational stamina — the amount of time they can attune themselves to exploring and relating their emotional expression. Even emotions like anger, which at first might appear to be challenging, can become less challenging and more familiar over time; eventually even shifting into new forms of healthy, empowering expression.

Instead of naming their feelings for them, we can intentionally make space for our children (or partners) to discover their own frames for what they are feeling, which can result in unexpected new insights. Perhaps, our children might choose to not name their feelings right away (another capacity building moment.) When a child is free to say, "I don't know what I feel right now but I may know later," they are essentially allowing time for what they feel to emerge. In this process, we keep them company while they find their way. We remain a steady presence.

We humans are complex. Sometimes what happens between us can't be named or understood immediately.

Children are perfectly capable of arriving at more layered views of human emotions when we make space for them to explore their relational capacities over time via ongoing conversations. In this process, our task is to keep them company and provide frames while they explore.

When we model for our children how to listen with curiosity, and how not to collapse into someone else's strong emotions, we are modeling a powerful form of emotional courage for them. In these moments, we are showing them it's okay not to know all the answers right away. It's okay to wait and see what emerges for us. It's a powerful way to listen to people. We are also showing our children that we trust who they are and the conclusions they will reach.

We can find ourselves genuinely surprised at their emotional acuity, saying, "Wow, I didn't think of that!" and, "Hey, I'm going to try that idea!" What can emerge in these moments is how emotionally astute our kids actually are.

> The process of growing our relational intelligence takes years. We, as parents, grow it in partnership with our children in the little, daily conversations of life.

The great joy here? These rich, little conversations about life and living, utterly distinctive and different for every family, create the closeness and connection we long for as parents.

Witnessing our children using their growing capacities to master life's challenges is deeply rewarding. The stronger, more resilient relationships that emerge for them are grounded in the joy of being authentically human.

Part six:

Language and meaning

IF YOU THINK ABOUT IT, EMOTIONS OFTEN APPEAR AS PHYSICAL SENSATIONS *IN OUR BODIES,* RIGHT? FOR INSTANCE, WE MIGHT FEEL A *SENSATION IN OUR GUT* OR WE MIGHT GET *SWEATY PALMS.*

BUT THEN, WE **NAME** THAT SENSATION, (PERHAPS BASED ON WHAT WE HAVE BEEN TAUGHT THESE SENSATIONS ARE SUPPOSED TO MEAN). WE MIGHT AUTOMATICALLY SAY **"I'M FEELING ANXIOUS"** WHEN WE'RE ACTUALLY FEELING LOTS OF THINGS, INCLUDING EXCITEMENT OR MAYBE UNCERTAINTY. OUR SENSATIONS HAVE **MANY POSSIBLE MEANINGS!**

SO, EMOTIONS MAY BEGIN AS SENSATIONS, THEN **LANGUAGE** COMES IN TO CREATE MEANING.

IMAGINE IF WE CHOSE **NOT TO NAME OUR FEELINGS RIGHT AWAY.** WE CAN EVEN SAY, "I DON'T KNOW WHAT THAT FEELING IS. I THINK I'LL SIT WITH IT A WHILE BEFORE I NAME IT."

SO LANGUAGE IS A POWERFUL PART OF HOW WE IDENTIFY OUR FEELINGS. IN LANGUAGE, WE GIVE MEANING TO OUR **EMOTIONS**...

...WHICH, IN TURN, CREATES OUR STORIES. **STORIES** THAT CAN BE HELPFUL OR UNHELPFUL TO US.

It isn't only what we say, it's the space we say it from.

Mark Greene

Part seven:

We live the stories we tell

WE CREATE OUR STORIES IN RELATIONSHIP TO OTHERS, OFTEN DURING MOMENTS WHEN WE HAVE **STRONG FEELINGS.**

WHEN OUR STORIES ARE CHARGED WITH EMOTION, THEY CAN FEEL LIKE *TRUTH* TO US, GIVING THEM A *POWERFUL INFLUENCE.*

AS WE HAVE SAID, OUR STORIES CAN BE **HELPFUL OR** THEY CAN CREATE **PROBLEMS.**

old stories

new stories

BUT EVEN BIG STORIES LIKE THIS CAN BECOME *HIDDEN FROM US OVER TIME.* SO MAYBE WE'RE BACK TO JUST FEELING THEM IN OUR GUT, KEEPING ALIVE THE SENSATION OF PAST EVENTS OR EMOTIONS.

BUT THEY ARE HAVING A BIG IMPACT, JUST THE SAME.

AFTER A TIME, I MIGHT REFRAME MY STORY AGAIN TO BECOME: **"I'M CONNECTING MORE WITH EVERYONE IN MY LIFE."**

REFRAMING IS THE WAY WE CAN **SHIFT** STORIES THAT ARE **CREATING PROBLEMS** FOR US.

THIS NEW STORY IS STILL A MOUNTAIN. IT WILL STILL REQUIRE OUR **COMMITMENT AND EFFORT** TO CLIMB, BUT THIS MOUNTAIN IS A PLACE OF **BEAUTY AND DISCOVERY** INSTEAD OF A THREAT.

BECAUSE *WE LIVE THE STORIES WE TELL,* FRAMING AND REFRAMING OUR STORIES ARE POWERFUL WAYS TO EMPOWER OURSELVES.

FIRST, WE *IDENTIFY* OUR STORIES

THEN, WE SEEK TO UNDERSTAND THEIR ROLE AS *HELPFUL OR UNHELPFUL.*

UNDERSTANDING THE STORIES WE CARRY ABOUT OURSELVES *AND OTHERS* IS THE KEY TO MAKING *CONSCIOUS CHOICES* IN OUR RELATIONSHIPS.

OUR CHILDREN ARE *IMAGINATION* SUPERSTARS!

IN A SINGLE AFTERNOON OF PLAY, OUR KIDS ARE ABLE TO STEP IN AND OUT OF *DOZENS OF STORIES,* EFFORTLESSLY.

SOME OF OUR CHILDREN'S STORIES ARE **EASY FOR US TO HEAR.**

BUT SOME OF OUR CHILDREN'S STORIES CAN BE QUITE *DIFFICULT FOR US TO HEAR.*

THE BOYS AND GIRLS AT THE PARK *DON'T LIKE ME!*

IF A STORY MAKES US UNCOMFORTABLE, WE MIGHT QUICKLY **SEEK TO CORRECT IT.**

THAT'S **NOT TRUE,** HONEY. LOTS OF KIDS AT THE PARK LIKE YOU.

WE MAY EVEN PRESENT *OUR PREFERRED STORY* TO END THE EMOTIONAL DISCOMFORT OUR CHILD'S STORY MAKES US FEEL.

YOU'VE GOT LOTS OF FRIENDS, ***OKAY?...***

OKAY... I *GUESS* SO...

BUT SIMPLY CORRECTING OUR CHILD'S DIFFICULT STORY CAN BE PRETTY ***UNSATISFYING*** FOR US AND OUR CHILD.

A VERY DIFFERENT PROCESS TAKES PLACE WHEN WE ENCOURAGE OUR LITTLE ONES TO TALK THROUGH THEIR CHALLENGING STORIES.

...THEN WE ALL WENT TO THE SWINGS AND I HAD TO *WAIT*...

WHEN WE INVITE OUR LITTLE ONES TO TELL THEIR STORIES, IT PROVIDES OPPORTUNITIES TO *RECONSIDER AND PERHAPS REFRAME EVENTS.*

99

THERE IS A WHOLE RANGE OF RELATIONAL SUPERPOWERS OUR KIDS CAN DEVELOP OVER THE YEARS THROUGH **CONVERSATION AND SELF-REFLECTION,** THE PROCESSES BY WHICH WE CONSIDER OUR VALUES AND BELIEFS IN THE WORLD.

THEY CAN LEARN TO:

SELF-REGULATE EMOTIONALLY

CARE FOR RELATIONSHIPS

APPRECIATE DIFFERENCE

MANAGE CONFLICT

GROW SELF-CONFIDENCE

RESIST PEER PRESSURE

EMPATHIZE

FORM COMMUNITY

THIS CAN BE THEIR STORY!

WHICH IS WHY STAYING **IN CONVERSATION** WITH OUR KIDS IS SO IMPORTANT. IT IS IN THE BACK AND FORTH OF RELATING THAT WE SHARE AND **CONSIDER** OUR STORIES AND BELIEFS.

Part eight:

The power of play

Welcome to the playground

Leading relational thinkers share the belief that who we are is constantly being redesigned and re-created amidst the back and forth of *relating* with others. To learn more, see the reading list at the end of our book. It includes works by Harlene Anderson and Kenneth Gergen.

When we commit to growing our relational capacities, we are in the process of co-creating who we are and who we are becoming. In a culture that often trains us to value consistency and control, how do we best engage the uncertainty generated by ongoing change and growth? It can seem unnerving.

> A singularly powerful way to engage ongoing change is to make the choice to stay playful, to improvise.

When we talk about staying playful, it can bring to mind playing games or being silly in childlike ways, but play represents a much broader and more intentional mindset. We can seek to hold our ideas or beliefs lightly, adopt a not-knowing position, be curious about the emergent, and seek to co-create new and different ways to look at the world in collaboration with our children or partner.

In choosing to be more playful, we can agree to explore and perhaps redesign our ideas or beliefs about life, relationships, parenting and more. When we look closely, we notice that even our most deeply held ideas and beliefs are not static. Context, relating, along with our own daily growth and change, evolves our beliefs and ideas.

Choosing to be more playful doesn't make ideas more flexible, it simply acknowledges that they already are.

In the moment we share an idea or belief, something new is already emerging. Think of a song performed by two different singers, or a dance step by two different dancers. We are performers, too.

In relationships, we each perform our distinctive versions of the ideas we share. This distinctiveness is deeply human and it is linked to why play is such a powerful creative force. In play, we welcome the generative nature of coordinating divergent ideas. And even better, in play, we intentionally hold our stories or beliefs more lightly. This expands the relational space as we allow ourselves to stay open and notice what is emerging in the dance of our distinctiveness. Play, in partnership with curiosity, transforms us into joyful learners and makers of our interconnected lives. It is the source of a wider range of options in how we go forward in life.

Children at play understand that their ideas are meant to co-exist with the ideas of others, giving rise to new ideas. In this way, the possibilities for play become endless. The source of our creativity isn't located in our ideas, but in the conversations they give rise to.

This is the central power of conversations. It is somewhere in the thousands of small daily conversations with our children that the eureka moments that grow our relational and emotional intelligence emerge. When we, as parents, ask instead of tell, hold uncertainty instead of seeking to fix, explore instead of insist, we expand the process by which young minds ask and answer many of their own questions, express and explore many of their own emotions.

Parents know that not everything can be up for discussion. Beliefs and rules must be put in place as a matter of safety or as moral and ethical absolutes. "Honor thy mother and father" is an example of a moral absolute many of us are committed to teaching our children. For the purpose of keeping our toddlers safe, "do not go in the street" is not up for debate.

But sometimes, we can find ourselves operating based on beliefs or rules we are not even fully aware of; rules we may have put in place long ago for reasons we no longer fully recall. These "half-aware" rules can assert a huge amount of influence over how we raise our children or interact with our partners. They may keep us from having adventures, seeking connection or taking risks. They can make us fearful or anxious.

When life becomes too much about rules, it can lose its joyful spontaneity.

When too many of our ways of being become rigid and inflexible, driven by schedules and deadlines and the business of daily living, relationships can falter. So, as important as the demands of the day are, we can also understand that parenting is not simply a role-based list of tasks; rather, it is an organic, breathing, relational space that we co-create in our interactions.

Being playful includes adopting what Harlene Anderson calls "a not-knowing stance." Anderson's work focuses on how we can offer guidance and knowledge, not as dictates, but as food for thought, thus opening up spaces for dialogue and co-creation.

Our beliefs about parenting are constantly evolving. Toddlers become teens. At some point, "do not go in the street" becomes "do not cross the street without looking both ways." As we grow our relational capacities, who our children are and what their relational strengths prove to be will determine which ideas need repeating and which ideas need to be revisited, revised, or set aside in order to move to the next level.

Our children demonstrate playful thinking every single day.

A box becomes a spaceship, piles of sand become castles. Children at play morph and swap out ideas minute by minute, holding none as sacred or absolute. How we respond to their call of imagination shapes their creativity.

With very young children, we might join them in their imagining. As they grow older we can keep asking, "How am I joining up with his or her imagination?" For instance, if we value college education, how might we respond when our 16-year-old declares "I'm not going to college after high school"?

How might we engage her declaration as an exploration rather than challenge it with a counter-declaration (a belief)? How might we see ourselves as entering a creative exploration? Children don't outgrow their fertile imaginations, we grow them out of imaginative thinking via our everyday responses.

When we continue to look at ideas and beliefs from different angles, in different contexts, and from different people's points of view, we help our children think about how we share and co-design our relationships through our ideas. These are pivotal moments of self-reflection, tied to a child's understanding of creativity as a playful social process.

We can encourage our children to explore and engage in playful ways, in the relational spaces we share with them. It is in this way that we can also engage and explore our own capacities, noticing what is emerging in relationship with others.

The playground is always there. And so, we have a choice each and every day. Along with all the goals and demands of daily life, we can also choose to regularly go back in time to the sunlit playgrounds of our youth and join our children there.

We can choose to *stay playful.*

Part nine:

The relational wheel

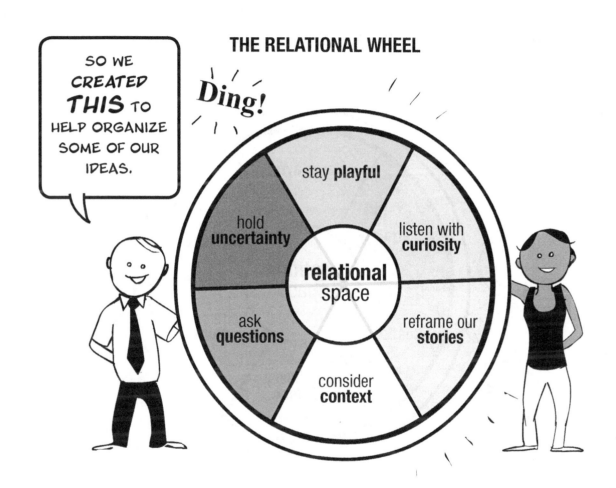

THE RELATIONAL WHEEL

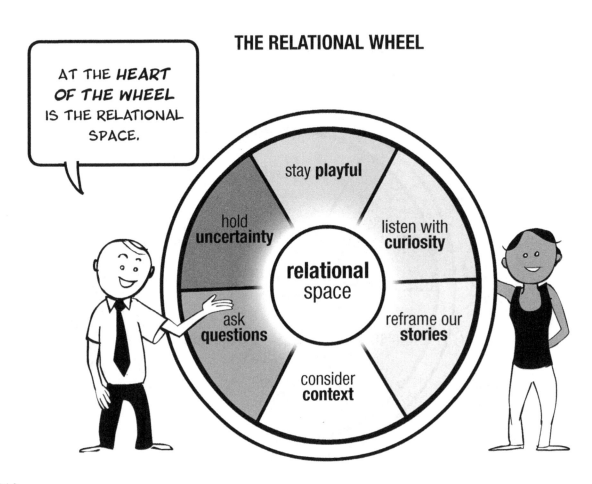

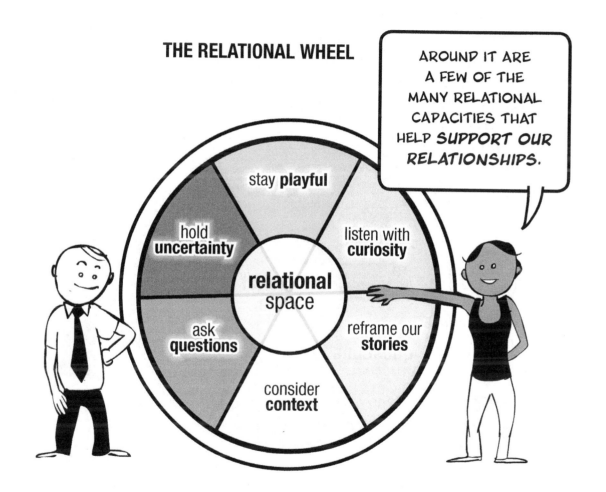

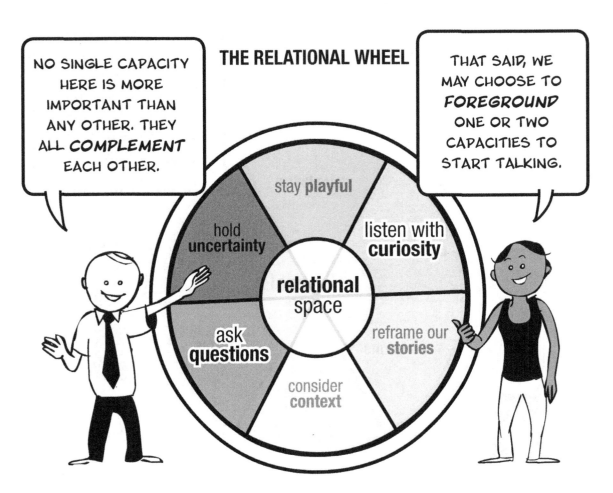

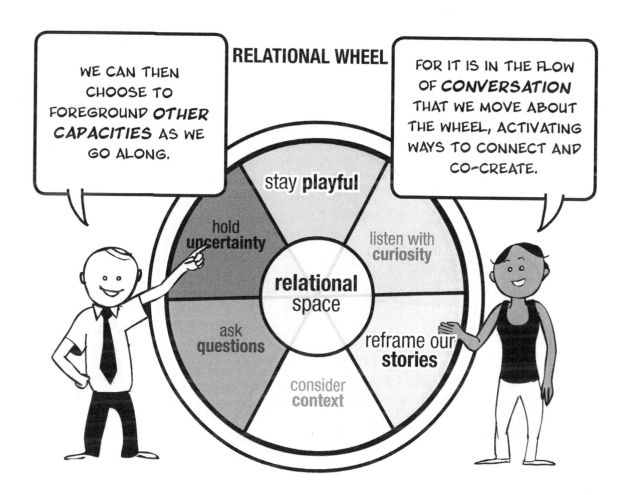

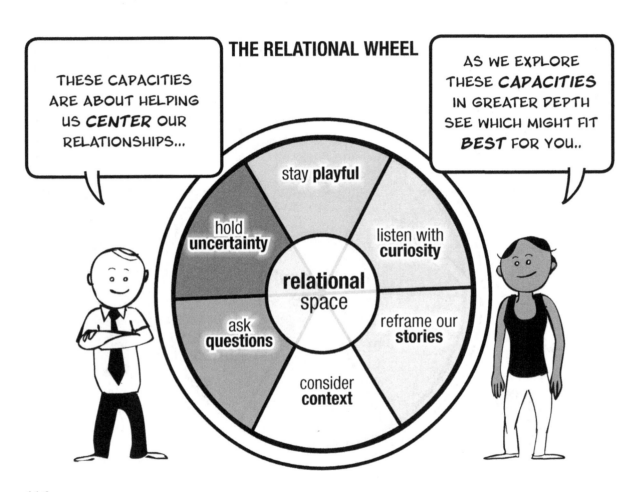

HOW DO WE LEARN TO SPOT RELATIONAL CAPACITIES OPERATING IN *DAILY LIFE?*

UP NEXT, MARK HAS WRITTEN THREE *FABLES* JUST FOR THIS PURPOSE. SEE IF YOU CAN SPOT RELATIONAL CAPACITIES AT WORK IN OUR THREE FABLES.

*The player is able to be in control
of being out of control and so enjoy a sense
of both risk and mastery simultaneously.*

Gwen Gordon & Sean Esbjorn-Hargens

Part ten:

Once upon a time ...

Inventing our own fables

Our friend Kristen grew up in Norway, a land rich in fables and folk tales. Now a grandmother, she tells a story of when she was a teen. She and her mother were going through a rough patch. One day, her father, who had told her many folk tales, began a story about a queen who very much wanted a daughter. He evoked the image of the queen, hoping beyond hope, pining for the child she feared she would never have.

As her father told the story, Kristen slowly realized this was not one of the fables other parents in Norway told their children. This folk tale was very special. It was for her alone. By the time she realized she was the princess in the story, and the queen was her mother, the deep and abiding love of the queen was already evident to her. Her father's fable shifted her thinking about her mother. So much so, that she remembers this powerful moment of rediscovering her mother's love for her, forty years later.

In 1990, family therapist Edwin Friedman wrote, "Fables, through the distance they provide, offer fresh perspective on familiar human foibles."As parents, we are constantly creating stories large and small. When we share them with our children, imparting the magic of imagination, our kids feel the joy of storytelling and the rich connection this embodies. Telling stories evokes play. It is the theater of life and it is magical.

We can tell our kids folk tales we remember from our childhood, or make up brand new stories of our own. In creating our own, we can share specific important messages or just enjoy silly, creative story energy which says to our children, "Imagination is fun!"

The process of storytelling is love. It is connection. And the stories we share may well get told to our great, great grandchildren.

***

In the following fables, look for moments of relational capacities at play. If you like, share these stories with your children, simply for fun, or as starting points to conversations about who we are and what we believe.

THE FABLE OF THE IDIOT PRINCE

Once, long ago, a king, a queen, a prince and a princess lived in a beautiful castle. The king and queen loved their children with all their hearts.

For years, they taught them all there was to know about the world. Coaches and tutors, teachers and priests paraded through the castle bringing the two children great and mysterious lessons about the world, lessons about how things worked and the history of who had made the world what it is.

Each night before they went to bed, the king and queen whispered to each as they fell asleep, "Who is one of the wisest young persons in the land? You are ...
Who is one of the most loved young persons in the land? You are ...
Who is one of the happiest young persons in the land? You are ..."

And then, one bright and sunny summer's day, just before his eleventh birthday, the young prince came home and announced, "I AM AN IDIOT!"

A shocked silence fell over the court. The big-screen TV at the end of the great hall was muted. All phones were switched to silent. And the castle dogs, sensing rough weather ahead, crawled under the great feasting table and fell silent, daring not even to scratch a flea.

The king cleared his throat. "My dear," he said to the queen, "I believe my hearing has failed me. I could swear the prince just declared himself an idiot."

The queen tipped her head to the side and smiled the way she always did when her husband was alarmed (not an uncommon occurrence) and replied, "Of course he didn't say that, my dear. He is the prince."

The boy studied them both. He tossed his head back and declared, "I'm a moron! A complete moron!"

The king sat up and removed his reading glasses.

"I beg your pardon," he said.

"I'm stupid," the boy said. "I'm very stupid."

The king and queen looked at each other, their eyes wide. The dogs beneath the great feasting table whimpered.

"You most certainly are not!" declared the king, his voice rising.

"My darling!" the queen said. "You are the smartest boy in the land!"

The prince looked at them both, a great sadness in his eyes. "I'm an idiot," he said again. "I'm a complete idiot."

The king became alarmed. What if someone heard the prince saying this? What if the villagers decided it was true? What if the prince became known as an idiot? What if HE become known as the father of an idiot? But most of all, he loved his son and knew him to be a thoughtful, intelligent child. Oh, it was all too much!

"I'll not have you saying that!" the king declared. "It's not right, you are very intelligent and you, of all people, know that to be true!"

When the boy heard his father's words, his shoulders slumped, his eyes dropped down and he looked defeated.

"I am an idiot," the prince repeated, looking more unhappy with each passing moment.

"Who told you this!" demanded the king.

"No one," the prince replied.

"Then how do you know it?" said the king.

"Because I'm an IDIOT!" the boy replied his voice rising. He raised his eyes and glowered at his father.

"Preposterous!" shouted the king. "If you insist on this absurd idea, you shall be banished to the digital dungeon of no internet until you change your mind! I'll simply not have it!"

The queen's fingers rose to touch her chin. She had a curious look in her eyes, as if listening to a voice no one else could hear.

And so, the battle raged as both father and son, who were each very strong-willed, refused to budge an inch. A day passed. Then two. The king tried every way he could think of to convince the prince that his dear son was no idiot. He cajoled, he declared, he insisted, he argued and ultimately he pleaded with his son to see reason.

"I'm an idiot!" declared the prince, bouncing a rubber ball.

"Absurd!" declared the king. "If you will not cease this ridiculous declaration, then I shall simply refuse to hear it. And that is that!"

Still the queen sat silently, the curious look in her eyes.

Another day passed. "I'm an idiot!" declared the prince.

"Balderdash!" the king responded. "Who will rid me of this terrible dilemma?" the king asked, worry creasing his brow. "I cannot order this to cease. I cannot convince our dear son to think better of himself. I cannot identify where this idea came from and I cannot wait it out."

The queen smiled, the curious look in her eyes, shining. She turned to the king. "I think I know who can help us," said the queen.

"Who?" the king asked.

"Call in the jester," she responded, smiling.

The king, was struck as if by a lightning bolt. Slowly a smile spread across his face, a very broad smile. "Of course!" he declared. "Bring in the royal jester!"

And the royal jester came. The prince, a glint in his eye, immediately turned to jester. Was it *amusement, anticipation?* Only the prince could say.

"Fair and beloved Prince," said the jester. "I hear you think yourself an idiot!"

The prince, bouncing his ball said, "I am an idiot. I am a moron. I am stupid."

"Wonderful!" declared the jester. "Fantastic! Exemplary!" shouted the jester. "I couldn't have said it better myself!" The jester capered about laughing with delight. "I cannot think of better words to describe you, most fair and beloved Prince!"

A shadow crossed the prince's face. Then, almost as quickly, the faintest of smiles. He cocked his head sideways, the way he did when playing chess.

"Really?" said the prince. "I AM an idiot?"

"A prince among idiots," replied the jester.

"I am stupid?" asked the prince, the smile creeping across his face.

"Most certainly," replied the jester.

"I'm a moron?" the prince asked, all his curiosity now focused on the jester.

"Without a doubt," replied the jester. He dropped to one knee, his eyes twinkling. He raised one finger, took a breath, and began.

"Idiot. I-D-I-O-T. You are an Intelligent, Delightful, Insightful, Open-hearted ..." the jester paused searching for the final word. "Thoughtful-er," declared the jester.

The prince paused. "That's just silly," he said, seeing the trick the jester had played.

"Words are silly," said the jester.

The prince paused. "Moron," he said, his eyebrows rising a bit.

"Oh my prince, that is almost too easy," said the jester. "M-O-R-O-N. Miraculous Offspring Realizing Optimal Nuance."

"Haw!" said the prince, "That's terrible!"

"T-E-R-R-I-B-L-E. Teaching Every Really Relatable Idea By Laughing Easily," said the jester with a shrug.

"No way," the prince declared, his eyes wide with surprise.

"That just leaves stupid," the jester noted.

The prince cocked his head again, like he did when playing chess.

"Simply Teaching Undermines Playful Insights Daily," the boy responded.

The jester leaned back, surprised in turn. "It does," he said. "It most certainly does," and with that, the jester took off his jester's hat and put his crown back on.

"Would you like to talk to me about what's going on?" said the king. "I'll just listen."

"I guess I could try" said the prince. "It's kind of complicated." With that, the prince began to tell his story.

THE FABLE OF FOXY-G

One fine summer evening, the prince told the king and queen a story and it went like this. There once was a fox named Foxy-G and he was the most elusive fox in the forest. One day, he would be standing on the high hill, the next day, deep in the woods and the next day, there he would be, by the river.

"How can we depend on you Foxy-G?" the other animals would say. "You're all over the map. We can't be sure of where you stand one day to the next," they said.

The hawk said to Foxy-G, "What is the point of being in the darkest parts of the forest? You can't fly there because of all the trees." He stamped side to side in disapproval.

"And why would you go near the rushing river," the squirrels asked Foxy-G. "There are no nuts there!" They flipped their tails with irritation.

"And who, in their right mind, stands on hills?" the mice asked Foxy-G. "The only thing to see there are predators swooping down on you! It's not safe. It's never safe!" they declared in high-pitched voices.

"We really must know where it is that you stand," all the animals declared.

And so it went, day after day, until Foxy-G's head was so full of different points of view that he began to wonder how many ways he could possibly be wrong. But every time he thought he might know where he stood, something new popped up to explore and he felt the urge to know just a bit more.

"Look at me," said the hawk. "I'm at home in the wide open. It suits me just fine. I can see everything. It's the best place to be. My choice is the best choice."

"It's really about understanding what's best," said the squirrels. "By the river is no place to be. There are no nuts there."

"We are not sure why you would stick your neck out like that," said the mice. "We animals are meant to be hidden. It's the best way of staying alive! Only the deep forest is safe. Really, things couldn't be simpler."

"Are you a river fox, a forest fox or a hilltop fox?" they demanded to know.

And so it went, month after month. Foxy-G began to feel guilty for all his wandering ways.

"If I go to the flowing river, the squirrels are not happy. If I explore the darkness of the forest, the hawk disapproves. And then, there are the mice. They are so fearful of being exposed, but I love the new things I can see from the hilltops," he muttered, as he explored along the edge of a pond in the woods.

"But each day that passes brings me no closer to deciding. I simply can't choose which place it is that I will belong." Foxy-G groaned. "What is wrong with me? Why am I so, so ... all over the place?"

Finally, pressure to decide just got to be too much, so, Foxy-G called a meeting of the animals to announce a decision. They met at an open glade in the forest.

"You have all convinced me," said Foxy-G. "I can no longer be a fox who is all over the map. It is time for me to decide what kind of fox I will be, otherwise, I'm just a fool who's nowhere at all."

At this point, the prince stopped telling his story to the king and queen. He looked at his father and mother. His eyes were sad. "I don't know what I think half the time. The other boys and girls are so sure of what they believe. They have such confidence. So, I pretend I know, but I don't know. My ideas don't seem ... finished. And so, I end up feeling like an idiot."

The king and queen sat with the prince. Then, after a time, the king simply said, "I feel that way too, sometimes. Like I see too many points of view."

"I know that feeling, too," said the queen.

The prince looked at them both, his sadness shifting perhaps a bit. "But you seem so sure of what you say," he said.

"Ah, well, there it is," his father said, smiling. "Seeing many points of view, doesn't mean you don't know what to do when the time comes."

The prince cocked his head sideways, the way he did when playing chess.

Then the queen said softly, "I heard something interesting in your story."

"Did you?" the prince said.

"I did," replied the queen. She waited.

The prince looked at her for a long moment, then a slow smile crept to his lips, so small a smile, that to not look for it was to not see it.

"What?" asked the prince.

"Oh, it's just something Foxy-G was doing," she replied.

"What?" the prince said, his voice rising.

"Well, you gave me an idea for the rest of the story," his mother replied.

"What?" said the prince.

"May I tell the rest of your story?" the queen replied.

"All right," said the prince, giving her his full attention because he loved his mother's stories.

And the queen began her part of the story.

So, Foxy-G was ready to make a decision about where he would stand in the world.

"You have all convinced me," he said. "It is time for me to decide what kind of fox I will be," said Foxy-G, but his tail, normally upright and full of energy, hung a little low.

The squirrels, the mice and the hawk murmured their agreement. "And what have you chosen," they asked him.

"I will let these three twigs decide," Foxy-G said, pushing three twigs toward them, two long and one short. He laid a leaf on top of them and said, "Each of you will reach under and pick one twig. Whomever picks the short twig will decide what kind of fox I am to be."

The animals murmured their agreement. "That suits us," said the squirrels. "We don't so much care what kind of fox you decide to be, it's simply high time you decide. Otherwise, it creates too much uncertainty for us."

"Unpredictability," said the hawk.

"Lack of clarity," said the mice.

And at that precise moment, a waft of smoke passed among the trunks of the trees.

"What is THAT?" declared the mice, twitching their whiskers.

"Is that smoke?" asked the hawk, his head high.

"Where is it coming from?" asked the squirrels their tails whipping in alarm. "What are we to do?"

"We must run!" said the mice.

"The hawk can tell us which way to go!" said the squirrels.

"I can look, but I do not know the way through the forest," said the hawk.

"We should burrow down here," said the mice.

"No, we should climb the trees," said the squirrels.

"Oh, dear! Hide! Hide!" they yelled, running in frantic circles.

"NO!" said Foxy-G. "We cannot stay here. We must leave this place. It is not safe here any more." He paused, thinking furiously, "We will go to the water. Only there will the fire pass by without harming us."

"What if the fire is between us and the river?" cried the squirrels.

"The current is too swift!" said the mice. "We will be swept away."

Meanwhile, the smoke was getting thicker. Somewhere in the distance they heard a crackling sound, but it seemed to be coming from more than one direction.

"That's it. I'm out," said the hawk, rising on his wings. "Good luck!" he cried down through the trees.

"Oh, how will we know where to run?" cried the mice.

"The river is that way," said Foxy-G. He turned his fine ears this way and that. "And so is the fire," he said.

"Oh, no! Oh, no!" cried the mice and the squirrels.

"Climb on my back," Foxy-G said to the mice as the sound of the fire grew. They climbed up on his back.

"Are you ready to run for your lives?" he asked the squirrels.

"We are!" cried the squirrels.

And Foxy-G took off running.

"This is not the way to the river!" cried the mice.

"I know," Foxy-G called out. "But I have taken many paths. I have seen many things.

I know the forest, the hillside and the river! And I see just a bit more!"

The squirrels raced alongside Foxy-G, running pell-mell as sparks floated about them. The roar of the approaching fire grew.

And suddenly, before them through the trees, was the pond. They raced into the calm, cool waters and swam out to the middle where a great log sat. They pulled themselves up, panting with exhaustion. They stayed there on the log in the pond and watched as the fire moved past like a great roaring beast through the trees. After a time, it was gone.

The animals swam back to the shore and pulled themselves up onto the bank.

"Don't decide where you stand," said the mice, panting still.

"Yeah, absolutely. Don't pick," said the squirrels, wide-eyed. "Don't you ever pick. You are Foxy-G and Foxy-G sees just a bit more."

And so he didn't pick. And to this day, no one knows where Foxy-G stands ... but they always trust him to know just a bit more.

And with that, the queen finished her story.

The prince looked at the king. The king raised his eyebrows, smiling but saying nothing.

"So," the prince said, "I'm Foxy-G?"

The queen smiled at her son. "What do you think?" she said.

THE FABLE OF THE CANDLE AND THE MOON

O ne night, the princess sat with the jester, looking out a high tower window. The sun had long since set. In the sky before them was the full moon. Far below, they could see the moonlit fields, the roads and rivers and forests, winding away into the distance.

"The moon is ancient. It has been in the sky since long before any living thing existed," said the princess.

"The moon is huge, greater in size than any mountain," said the jester.

"The moon is beautiful," said the princess. "It is the subject of countless songs and poems and stories."

"The moon inspires passion in lovers, young and old," said the jester.

"Ew," said the princess, making a face.

"Well, it does," said the jester. "Someday you'll appreciate that."

"At night, the full moon is the most powerful source of light in the world."

"Yes, it is," said the jester. "Except when it's not."

"Oh, here we go again," said the princess, rolling her eyes.

The jester took a nearby candle and holding it before the princess said, "How mighty by comparison is this humble candle?"

The princess scoffed. "I can blow it out with one breath. Can I blow out the moon?"

"Close your eyes," said the jester.

The princess closed her eyes and smiled. "The moon is gone, but the candle is not. I can still see its light. All right then, but you cannot deny that the moon moves the mighty oceans. That is a power you cannot deny."

"Score one for the moon," said the jester. "But I would ask you this. Can the moon wound you? Because I assure you if you hold your finger in this flame ..." the jester said.

"Score one for the candle," said the princess. "But I need only step away from the candle to be safe. The moon's power spans the world."

"True enough," said the jester. "But what if I do this?" The jester held the candle up in the window. Its bright, flickering flame blotted out the moon.

"Now I cannot see the moon, nor the stars, nor the night," admitted the princess.

"And think one step further," said the jester. "Can you move the moon to your purposes?" He moved the candle before him in a slow circle, their shadows dancing a pirouette.

"No," said the princess. "I admit, I cannot."

The jester rose. "Come with me away from the window," said the jester.

The princess followed. The jester blew out the candle, plunging the room into darkness. "I can only see the pool of moonlight on the floor," said the princess.

"Would you like for me to relight the candle?" said the jester.

There was a moment of silence.

"Yes, I think so," said the princess.

"Why is that?" said the jester. "Are you afraid of the dark?"

"No," said the princess, "I would simply like to see your face."

"Score one for the candle," said the jester as he struck a match and lit it. In the glow of its light, he smiled.

"So, since we have to choose," said the jester. "Is the candle or the moon more powerful?"

"Hmmm," said the princess. "I'm not sure. Do I have to choose? They are both very powerful," she said, "But it would seem the candle is the winner. For without it, I cannot see my own family."

"I'm with you. Why must we decide these things, anyway?" the jester responded. "I never settle my mind on anything. That's why I am a fool. Come with me," he said, and carrying the candle, he walked down the long staircase to the courtyard below. The candle lit their way to the main gate, where a soldier stood guard.

"Please open the gate. The princess and I would like to take a walk," said the jester.

"I'm sorry," said the guard, "but the king has forbidden the princess to be outside the walls after dark."

The jester was startled, then he laughed to himself. He removed his jester's hat and put on his crown.

"Your majesty, I did not see you there," said the guard, opening the gate.

"Thank you for doing your duty," said the king to the guard.

The king then removed his crown and replaced his jester's cap. The jester and the princess walked out into the nighttime fields surrounding the castle.

"And now, about this most powerful candle," said the jester. "We will use it to spy out the rabbits, foraging at the far edge of the fields." The jester looked and saw nothing. He turned to the princess. "I'll try and hold it higher." The jester stood on tiptoes, "Still. Not. Working ..." said the jester, stretching as high as he could.

The princess raised one eyebrow. "All right," said the princess. "Your point is made." The jester blew out the candle and the nighttime fields leapt into visibility, awash in the light of the full moon.

"The candle in the castle is very different than the candle in the nighttime fields," said the princess.

"Is very different than the candle in the nighttime fields without a full moon," said the jester.

"Ugh!" scowled the princess. "Will this never end? This compared to that, compared to this, compared to that. It drives me crazy, sometimes."

"Me, too," said the jester.

They stood in silence looking out at the fields. As the minutes passed and their eyes became accustomed to the dim moonlight, details began to emerge from farther and farther away.

"Score one for the moon," murmured the princess. "And the candle would have made it impossible to spot them." There in the distance, they could see rabbits grazing at the edge of the field. Occasionally, each rabbit, in turn, would raise up and look about, then drop back down to nibble on the fresh clover that grew there.

The princess and the jester watched wisps of clouds sweep across the moon. They heard the calls of night birds. A breeze rose and fell. It was a beautiful night.

"So, out here," said the princess, "the candle has less importance, but in the rooms of the castle, the moon is of less consequence. So power lies neither in the moon nor the candle," said the princess, puzzling out the answer.

"The power of either is determined by where we are in the kingdom," the princess said.

The jester's smile was faint in the moonlight. "Very good! But know this. What things mean to us is more than just where we are standing. It is many things. Shall I change the importance of the candle in an instant?"

"Just when I thought I had the answer, father!" laughed the princess. "Please do."

The girl's father removed his jester's cap and put on his crown. "Guard! Please join us in the field for our walk!" shouted the king.

"Yes, my lord," responded the distant guard. "Where are you, my lord?"

The princess smiled. She took the matches from her father and lit the candle.

"Ah, there you are, my lord and lady!" called the guard, heading their way.

"Score one for the candle," said the princess, laughing.

Part eleven:

The fables and the wheel

THE RELATIONAL WHEEL

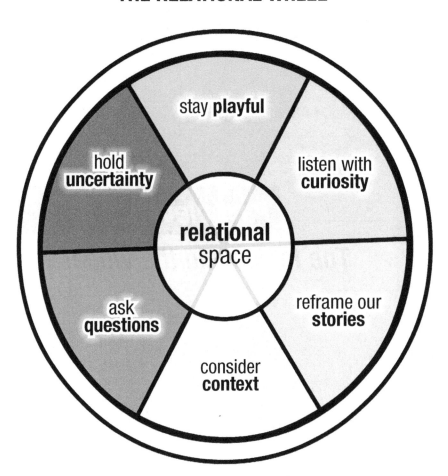

The Relational Wheel

Think of our Relational Wheel as a spinner on a board game, designed to encourage different ways to engage in conversation with others. On this Relational Wheel are six practices that can enhance our capacities for relating. They are important ideas, but it is the conversations they give rise to that matter most, because conversation is central to our connection and creativity. Conversation is relating *and relating is the activity by which we co-create relationships.*

Relationships have no starting point. All relationships are informed by those that intersect with it and those that preceded it, even back across generations. At birth, we are born out of relationships into relationships.

Compassion, empathy, love, sadness, grief and loneliness; every idea, aspiration, plan, goal and product; every human belief and experience is co-created in relationships.

> We are the product of thousands of relationships over a lifetime. How we relate in relationships creates who we are becoming.

Even as we walk alone in a park our relationships go with us. People we have not seen in years continue to inform who we are as we grow and change and reflect on our time with them. Grandmothers and grandfathers who have passed on, childhood friends

149

long gone; all remain a part of our growth and change. In this same way, parenting is not limited to the parent-child relationship. Every relational moment, both good and bad, is rooted in the larger network of relationships we are all embedded in.

To care for one relationship, we must care for them all.

We live in a world that often focuses on techniques as solutions. Accordingly, it is rare for us to consider the difference between a technique and an intention, but this distinction is central to growing our relational intelligence.

There are many capacities mentioned throughout this book. Some are on the Relational Wheel, some are not. They are all equally valid, and each is more helpful when held as an intention rather than a technique. As in, "It is my intention to be playful. It is my intention to acknowledge offers."

An intention *represents a practice for how to be with others over time* rather than a technique we are applying in the moment. Relational thinking helps us make the conscious choice to center our relationships. The fundamental moral premise we highlight in that moment is the difference between power created with others versus power created over others. Joyous, authentic social connection has been shown to improve and prolong our lives. Power with others, located in communities of healthy, vibrant relationships, is where we find security, resiliency, connection and support.

We can choose to foreground any capacity on the Relational Wheel — that is, momentarily emphasize it above the others. Relational capacities can overlap, grow, and complement each other. We can foreground multiple capacities at the same time without them coming into conflict with each other.

For example, foregrounding our intention to stay playful may also activate holding uncertainty. There is overlap between these two capacities. Our goal may be to try and connect without worrying about what comes next; to let go of lists and plans and schedules for the moment, and just be in connection with our child or partner. Holding uncertainty might make us curious, which in turn might help us let go of our worries. For the moment, we may frame our story as "We will get everything done. For now, let's connect."

Once we are connecting, we might shift and foreground listening, which in turn invites us to ask more questions. Our intention might be to see our child or partner with fresh eyes, listening for new developments in how they view life. We use our intuition to guide our choices as we move around the wheel.

In a moment of crisis, the choice to foreground staying playful may mean something very different than during a time of ease. In the case of a challenging event or issue, we may switch back to foregrounding holding uncertainty as a way to avoid reactivity, hang in with our child, and be with them as they share their stories.

Relational capacities operate in uniquely different ways depending on context. In our comic strip, we see how listening with curiosity operates in one way between Mark and Saliha (two adults), and another way between Mark and Bobby (an adult and a child).

Between Mark and Saliha, listening with curiosity helps both of them to set aside their unhelpful stories in order to connect; while between Mark and Bobby, the same capacity helps Mark make space for his son's ideas to grow.

As we take them on as intentions, relational capacities become second nature to us. They can shift who we are, redefining the culture we are creating. Relational capacities operate in the interplay between people. What is created emerges in the back and forth of relating. Good or bad, what emerges is always co-created and co-designed.

All parents hold uncertainty. All parents play. All these capacities are already active in hundreds of millions of homes across the world. We present the Relational Wheel as a sort of cheat sheet, a simple reminder of ways we can engage relational spaces.

If we're feeling stuck, we can take a look at the wheel and pick a way to shift the conversation and bring the focus back to how we are relating. This ongoing intention to focus on relationships holds a powerful promise: *It is what ultimately can get us unstuck in all aspects of life.*

When we choose as parents to shift our focus from performing the role of a parent to being in relationship with our children, we shift from acting on our children to acting with our children. This shift moves our children from being a product of our parenting to them being in relationship with us.

This distinction may seem like a trick of language, but it is in relationship with us that our kids will grow the relationship superpowers they need to succeed. Our goal is not just to achieve the markers of successful parenting, grades, behavior, appearance, manners. The deeper lessons of how to be in relationship with others are first learned with us.

> What are we teaching our children? Do we act on others, or do we co-create and co-design *with* them?

This is the central question of how we can choose to be human. The first path leads to isolation. The second holds the key to connection, collaboration, and innovation, bringing meaning, fulfillment, and joy.

There is no isolated self or fully private experience. Rather, we exist in a world of co-constitution. We are always already emerging from relationship; we cannot step out of relationship; even in our most private moments we are never alone.

Kenneth J. Gergen

NOW, LET'S EXPLORE THE SIX CAPACITIES ON OUR **RELATIONAL WHEEL** BY SEEING HOW THEY SHOW UP IN OUR FABLES.

THERE IS A LOT GOING ON **RELATIONALLY** IN OUR FABLES. WE'RE NOT TRYING TO FIT EVERYTHING IN HERE. WHAT **ADDITIONAL INSTANCES** DO YOU SEE?

Stay playful

The capacity to stay playful does many things at once. It invites us to step away from teaching and telling and instead give in to playful improvisation and co-designing of what is emerging. Additionally, play allows us to engage the to-do lists and tasks of daily life in a lighter-hearted way. Play infuses creativity. It is not the opposite of work, it is a more joyful way of working. We don't refuse the work of life, we change the place we approach it from. Play accesses the multiple parts of ourselves, helps us let go of fixing problems and instead live into co-creating. Play serves to shift our focus to the activity of connecting as we do the work of living.

We can also adopt the playful capacity as our "way of being with" in times of crisis and challenging emotional upheaval. Along with capacities like listening with curiosity, witnessing, and holding uncertainty, play helps us to not collapse into the emotions of our loved ones, but instead create a listening/holding space so they can process and share what is emerging for them.

In the fables:

In *The Fable of the Idiot Prince,* the prince declares himself an idiot, stupid and a moron. The king becomes reactive, opposing his son's statements, showing disapproval and frustration until he is reminded of the power of play by the queen. He then shifts, responding playfully in several ways.

When the king accesses a more playful persona (the jester) he and the prince engage a different side of their relationship. Staying playful overlaps with the capacity to hold uncertainty. In engaging his jester self, the king sets aside his fears and reactivity about his son's statements. In turn, this reduction in reactivity makes his son more receptive to sharing his thoughts and discovering alternative ideas.

Secondly, the king chooses to stop reacting to words like "idiot" and instead chooses to play with their meanings. The choice to hold his reactivity more lightly is the jester's unspoken acknowledgment to his son that the king is willing to shift his own reactions. A more co-creative space emerges, allowing them to move forward and explore the prince's stories together.

In activating his capacity to stay playful, the king shifts:
- how he is relating with his son
- his relationship with his own reactivity
- his relationship with the meaning of words

In *The Fable of the Candle and Moon,* we see how context creates meaning. It is in playful exploration of context that the jester shows the prince how we can look at our ideas from many angles.

Adopting a more playful mindset leads to flexibility, possibilities, innovative problem solving, collaborative capacities and even increased ability to hold empathy for others.

Listen with curiosity

When we listen to win an argument, or prove our point, the process is very different than when we listen to provide a holding space for the stories and emotions of others. When we give our loved ones a space to express what they are feeling without offering solutions, reactivity or judgments, it can be a life-affirming moment for both parties. In some cases, simply being heard is all a loved one or friend needs to create new emotional expressions and new meanings for their experiences.

It's easy to see how the capacity to listen with curiosity overlaps with the ask questions capacity, but the capacity to hold uncertainty is equally relevant here. Holding the intention to listen with curiosity invites us to set aside our stories, expectations and histories with others. We instead can listen with a beginner's mind, with the expectation we will be pleasantly surprised by new discoveries and ideas in the conversation we are entering into. Setting our stories aside takes us from certainty to uncertainty, and it opens up the back-and-forth to new possibilities.

When we operate from a place of certainty, we sometimes can forget that all conversations have multiple threads, multiple possibilities for where the conversation can go next. Which threads we choose to notice and engage determines where those conversations will go. We can choose to reach out and grab the thread that reinforces our frustrations, fears, or assumptions, or we can be curious about other threads that may offer new ideas or possibilities that could create substantive change.

In the fables:

In *The Fable of the Idiot Prince*, the king and the prince are at an impasse. Neither will budge from their positions. Perhaps the prince wants to push back against his parents' simplistic optimism about him in what, for him, is an increasingly complex world. Perhaps the king is not ready to see his son give up his childhood innocence. Whatever the reasons, the two are stuck.

In order to break the impasse, one of the two needs to let go of their position or approach it from a different direction. Shifting to the playful presence of the jester activates the jester's capacity to hold uncertainty, but it is the king's offer to "just listen" that removes the tension his son is feeling about sharing his experiences.

When we offer to listen without a rush to take action, others can often share what they are struggling with, create new meanings and feel supported. This simple idea may be one of the most powerful on the wheel.

Reframe our stories

As human beings, we carry stories about ourselves and others. These stories can be personal, familial, socio-political, cultural, and historical. Stories are the meanings we give to a lifetime of experiences that shape who we are, what we seek, how we see the world and how we engage with others. Stories come alive in our relationships.

Stories can be helpful or problematic, depending on our contexts and relationships. They can impact how we listen to others, sometimes determining what we think of their motivations and ideas before they even have an opportunity to share what they are thinking and feeling. If we are not aware of our stories, they can have a powerful influence on how we are relating even while remaining hidden away from us.

In the fables:
In *The Fable of Foxy-G,* we meet a young fox who is in the process of constructing his story of himself. Like most young people, his story is forming, and so it can look like one of self doubt or confusion, especially when contrasted by a community which is demanding clarity of him.

This idea of knowing who we are and having a clearly defined purpose is a powerful one in many cultures, including ours in the United States. Boys and girls feel the pressure to model confidence and clarity, even when their internal stories may be in turmoil or transition. While confusion is not typically valued in Western cultures, it exists right alongside of not-knowing and uncertainty, two frames that we argue here are positive and empowering. We, as parents, can choose to reframe confusion as not-knowing, an energetic generative space in which our children and ourselves are processing change and creating our next story.

In our fable, Foxy-G successfully holds his uncertainty about what kind of fox he will be and continues to explore. This can be seen as strength of character. Sometimes our stories are reframed incrementally through conversation and self-reflection over time. In a case like Foxy-G's, our stories about ourselves can change in an instant, when an event shifts the context in which we are being viewed (and judged).

In both *The Fable of the Idiot Prince* and *The Fable of Foxy-G,* we see the prince sharing his own internal confusion as well. A fable like *Foxy-G* is a good way to begin a conversation with our children about the stories they carry in their own lives.

Finally, in *The Fable of the Candle and the Moon,* we see the prince's story about who he is shifting in more subtle ways. When we invite our children to play with complex ideas, we create the story for them that they are members of the community of creative thinkers.

The capacity to reframe our stories invites us to examine and, when needed, shift or set aside stories that might be getting in our way.

Consider context

The capacity to consider context invites us to track stories, events, and ideas around us that impact the meaning of what we are experiencing. Contexts can be emotional, familial, social, cultural, historical, situational, geographical and more.

We can understand context this way. Imagine a conversation taking place in two different situations about a challenge a couple is having in their relationship. Scenario one, a couple has just finished receiving one-hour massages at a spa. Scenario two, the same couple has just battled their way through holiday shopping crowds for six hours. In which scenario do you think the couple will have a more generative conversation about their challenge? If you said scenario one or are thinking "it depends," both acknowledge context. And both may be right.

Clearly, context can be thought of as present events that affect our tone, mood, level of energy and more. But context is also our histories, our fears and the cycle of events we are creating. In order to consider context, we must consider how the multitude of events and experiences we encounter daily intersect. It is a cycle of meaning by which context defines our goals or actions, which in turn, redefine context and so on.

In the fables:
The Fable of the Candle and the Moon shows ways in which context can make relative what we might at first determine to be more concrete or factual. The fact (Ha ha!)

is, almost any belief or idea can have multiple meanings for us. In *The Fable of the Candle and the Moon*, the power of the candle is impacted by these contexts and more:

- location: inside or outside the castle
- intention: what the prince or jester seeks to do
- relationships: how those around the prince impact what he focuses on

We take in a vast range of factors when we consider context. Doing so mindfully is empowering. Being unknowingly buffeted by context is disempowering. We need to be conscious of how both mood and meaning shift depending on context, thereby granting context a powerful influence as we are relating.

The jester helps the prince see the power of context by being playful with a logic problem. Not only does the prince see the presence of context in factors like location, he also sees how more subtle contextual factors, like the choice to be playful, can affect how we relate to each other and form our beliefs.

Becoming aware of context empowers our relational choices. It can allow us to more fully understand what drives our actions and the actions of others.

Ask questions

The capacity to ask questions invites us to hear the ideas and opinions of others. Questions can evoke resourcefulness, grow perspective, open up conversations, help us make meaning, develop understanding of context, and much more. When questions cease to serve as demands for answers, and instead serve to encourage the back and forth of relating, they become powerful resources.

In even the simplest conversations, our minds often tend to race ahead, filling in the gaps and making assumptions about what goes unspoken. The capacity to ask questions overlaps with the capacity to listen with curiosity, both of which can be encouraged when we are willing to hold uncertainty. When we ask questions, listen, and stay in the creative tension of not knowing, we are able to see new ideas emerging with our child or partner.

The tone of our questions is also important.
Question: "Why did you do that?"
Same question stated differently: "Can you tell me more about why you did that, so I can better understand?"

These are two very similar questions, but their tone is a world apart. How we ask questions broadcasts our state of mind. Is it a judgmental question or a curious one?

Are we open to learning something new from this person or have we already made up our minds about what their response will likely be? Additionally, in the case of emotionally charged circumstances, we can even precede our question by first asking permission. "May I ask you a question?" In seeking permission to ask, we check in on how they are feeling about talking further. It is a courtesy that creates a more receptive climate because it genuinely allows for a "No."

In the fables:

In *The Fable of the Idiot Prince*, the king asks his son, "Would you like to talk to me about what's going on?" He then follows it with this statement, "I'll just listen." The king is signaling his intent to listen without jumping in. The king is acknowledging previous times when he may have been more opinionated while his son told his story. As such, the king is signaling he will stay in the more listening space and give the prince time to perhaps create new ideas about what he is feeling.

In *The Fable of Foxy-G*, the queen completes her son's story, but she does so only after asking him for permission to do so. It is a gesture of collaboration. Her influence is rooted in her history of storytelling with her son, but she activates the prince's receptivity when she asks for his permission. Asking permission is a singularly powerful relational moment because when the answer is yes, it activates a receptive mindset.

Questions are a powerful way to invite unspoken ideas and open up dialogue, but questions are subject to context, tone, and intention.

Hold uncertainty

Sometimes, for parents, our urge to fix things can be born out of our own discomfort with our children's emotional turmoil. We fix what we feel is causing our child's distress and then we say, "There, it's fixed," meaning *don't show me your turmoil any more.* In the rush to resolve our discomfort, we eliminate the back and forth of relating.

Children learn the complex art of making meaning in the back and forth of relating with others. This back and forth can be uncertainty inducing, but the process becomes generative when we learn to:

- shift our way of being by tracking and acknowledging context
- present our questions as food for thought
- take action by focusing on the relationship in addition to outcomes
- stay playful

The capacity to hold uncertainty invites us to take our focus off fixing problems and immediately providing answers. When we instead focus on what emerges if we stay in the creative space of not knowing, we give our children time and space to create their own solutions. Typically, uncertainty doesn't get conceptualized as a potential resource. We are often taught to avoid or eliminate it. But holding uncertainty is a great resource to open up possibilities for ourselves and our children.

In the fables:

In *The Fable of the Idiot Prince,* the king becomes immediately frustrated rather than holding the complexity of the prince's declarations and exploring further.

How is the jester holding uncertainty in ways that the king can not? Perhaps the prince is entering a new phase of more complex thinking about his role in the world? Perhaps the prince is about to make a developmental leap, preceded by a period of turmoil? What if some form of social awareness is driving the prince's ideas?

One big fear the king may be holding is that his son's innocence is suddenly slipping away. But what if the jester views it instead as a powerful new evolution in his son's thinking that simply needs companionship and positive frames to help it along?

What's more, in times of emotional turmoil, we can also provide the powerful capacity to hold uncertainty on behalf of other adults, and when personally confronting our own challenges.

When we activate our capacity to hold uncertainty, we allow for the emergence of new frames that arise in the back and forth of connection, allowing us to engage the issue at hand with agility. Our children can rely on our shared relational space as a container to play with their emotions, allowing them to process and ask questions as we create new meanings and actions together.

Do I contradict myself?
Very well, then I contradict myself,
I am large, I contain multitudes.

Walt Whitman

Part twelve:

Games and small conversations

Ongoing conversations

When parents have something significant we want to communicate to our children, we can be tempted to have a "big talk." In the case of talking about challenging emotions, this can be an even more difficult conversation than most. Where to start? What to discuss? How to get kids to open up at all?

Which brings us to games and play. As we play games, we carry on conversations that explore the way the game is operating, what it reminds us of, who is doing what and all sorts of other subjects unrelated to the game itself. These are small conversations, happening amidst play. How important are these small conversations?

If we pause and think for a moment, much of the meaningful work of parenting happens in the small daily conversations that take place when walking to school or getting ready for bed. And it is in the small daily conversations that our ideas about life are explored.

Conversations, large or small, encourage our learning how to self-reflect. The Merriam-Webster dictionary defines self-reflection as "careful thought about your own behavior and beliefs."

When a child is first invited to talk about something like strong emotions, it may seem awkward or even alarming for all involved. But we can prepare for challenging emotional talks by encouraging little moments of self-reflection to take place in our small daily conversations. In small conversations, important issues weave in and out of other seemingly unrelated subjects.

Furthermore, almost any topic can advance self-reflection if we just ask "So, how are you thinking and feeling about THAT?" When we invite our children to self-reflect in small daily ways, we begin putting relational language and frameworks in place that make these kinds of conversations possible in more emotionally charged moments.

Even in a challenging moment, our kids might say "Oh, this is how we talk about emotions," or "This is how dad or mom asks questions about emotions."

Because of how kids respond to "big conversations" (they often don't), small conversations help to grow our kids' relational stamina. Relational stamina refers to their ability to hang in with deeper conversations about their emotions and relationships. Small conversations acclimate our children to emotional self-reflection much more effectively than trying to force one or two big conversations. Small conversations can be very effective if we focus on asking curious questions, leaving lots of space for our child to come up with their own ideas.

Parent: Did you see Danny today?

Child: Yes, he was at recess. He tried to grab the ball.

Parent: What did you think when he did that?

Child: I got mad.

Silence. Walking.

Child: He does it to everybody.

Parent: How come?

Child: I don't know.

Silence. Walking.

Child: Maybe he doesn't know how to be friendly?

CHILD'S IDEA EMERGING!

Parent: Could be.

AND ... cut. The conversation moves on to something else. Legos, perhaps.

These small conversations fly under the infamous "kid radar." Kid radar tracks when we, as parents, have some specific message we feel we need to communicate. They know when "I want to talk with you" means "I want you to do something differently." And sometimes, that kind of conversation needs to happen, but we can choose to mix it

173

up; not always be prescriptive, offering solutions right out of the box.

The magic of small conversations is that they are less focused on teaching and telling and more focused on relating. It is in the back and forth of relating that information is shared and new ideas are born. Small conversations create spaces where our children have time to come up with their own observations and ideas. Especially if we listen with curiosity and don't jump in to give answers.

So, we can track the moments when our child may ask a question or share a feeling or observation. We can stay curious. We can follow it up with a question of our own. If we have something we want to share, we can try getting buy-in before we share it. Perhaps something like:

"I have a couple of ideas why I think that happened. Can you guess what one is?"

We can make an observation and move on through. "Maybe Danny was feeling embarrassed, so he just acted mean at the playground to cover that up."

Ultimately, we may discover our children starting these small self-reflective conversations themselves. How do we encourage this? The following are a number of games and ideas designed to prompt the conversations, large and small, that grow our relational intelligence.

The conflict game

Our young son (age five at the time) was seeing every serious discussion his parents had as a "fight." We were a blended family. Saliha is our son's "bonus mom." Our son had already witnessed his birth mother and father choosing to end their marriage. So, he began to worry even if his bonus mom and dad simply debated an issue. This created genuine concern for him. For him, any level of debate equaled having a fight, and fighting might mean the end of marriages.

We came to realize the issue had become central for him, so we created a simple theater game we called the Conflict Game. We sat our son down and told him we were going to be actors and portray a conversation. Then we performed a disagreement about something simple, in this case, what to have for dinner.

For the first example, Mark chose to act a little annoyed but not to raise his voice. Saliha wanted hamburgers. Mark wanted spaghetti. Then we turned to our son and asked, "Was that a conversation, a discussion, a debate, a disagreement, an argument, or a fight?" (The answer was a discussion with a bit of annoyance on the side.) Then we replayed the same discussion with raised voices. We asked him again, "Was that a conversation, a discussion, a debate, a disagreement, an argument, or a fight?"

"I don't know," he said. "A disagreement, maybe an argument?" In that moment, he began parsing out levels of disagreement, something he had never done before.

Then we asked him to take his dad's place and play out the game again. He leapt at the opportunity to play a character. (The power of play was on full display.) He secretly selected, in partnership with Saliha, what level of disagreement they wanted to perform. Mark's job became to identify correctly which level was being portrayed.

Our son came out portraying a person in a very angry argument, but he kept collapsing into laughter, too. Then, Mark replaced Saliha, and our son and his dad portrayed a different conversation, this time about what to do at the park. It was spoken like Englishmen having a snobby debate.

Each time, a determination was made. Each time the three of us decided whether we had portrayed a conversation, a discussion, a debate, a disagreement, an argument, or a fight.

In this game, our son performed various levels of conflict. He also modeled conflict with his own parents. These two experiences helped him develop a wider range of choices about how to express and interpret disagreements.

We talked about the differences between levels of disagreement. We talked about which approaches are most likely to lead to a resolution and which are likely to lead to more fighting. We talked about how to lower the level of our reactions in life. We talked about how, when we do have a fight that feels angry or mean, we can come back and make it right, because fights happen and it is what we do afterwards that is most important. Powerful stuff.

Our son liked the conflict game. It was a lot of fun pretending to be annoyed, or snobby, or indifferent. Over the following years, we played it many times. Even in the middle of heated family discussions.

"Why are you mad, Dad?"
"I don't think I'm mad. Maybe I'm just frustrated, or annoyed."
"How would I know which, Dad?"
"Okay, well, you and Saliha show me how I look. Let's play the Conflict Game."

And so on.

- How do you perform conflict in your family?
- How does your family talk when someone gets upset or angry?
- How does your family make up or resolve conflict?
- What is your message to your children about being angry?

SO INSTEAD, MAYBE WE ASK *QUESTIONS* ABOUT ANGER? "ON A SCALE OF ONE TO TEN, HOW ANGRY WERE YOU?"

WAIT! *I KNOW!* WE ASK "WERE YOU FEELING ANNOYANCE, IRRITATION, FRUSTRATION, OR ANGER?"

WHICH MEANS EVEN IF WE *DON'T LIKE* EXPLORING ANGER, WE KIND OF NEED TO FIGURE OUT WHY WE'RE MAD, *RIGHT?*

THEN WE COULD TALK ABOUT THEIR ANSWERS: "A LEVEL SIX? SO YOU WERE JUST KIND OF ANGRY?" OR "SO, THERE ARE *LEVELS* OF ANGER?"

ANGER CAN COVER UP A BUNCH OF *DIFFERENT* FEELINGS, RIGHT?

...AND AT WHOM. OURSELVES? SOMEONE ELSE? IS IT A VALID REASON? IS IT HIDING SOME OTHER *FEELINGS?*

LIKE SHAME, OR EMBARRASSMENT, DISAPPOINTMENT, LOSS OR FEAR OF REJECTION... THE LIST CAN BE *LONG...*

AND HOW DO WE PERFORM BEING ANGRY? DON'T FORGET *THAT PART,* HOW WE EXPRESS ANGER...

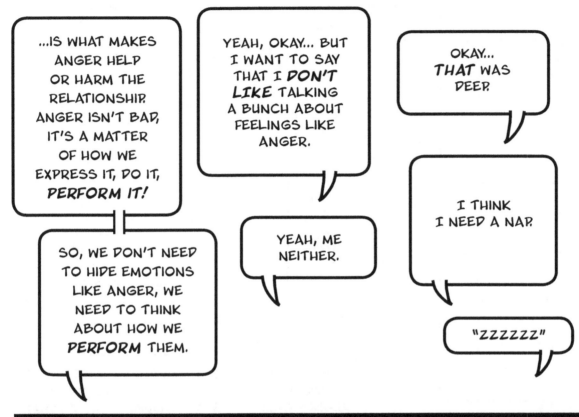

...IS WHAT MAKES ANGER HELP OR HARM THE RELATIONSHIP. ANGER ISN'T BAD, IT'S A MATTER OF HOW WE EXPRESS IT, DO IT, **PERFORM IT!**

SO, WE DON'T NEED TO HIDE EMOTIONS LIKE ANGER, WE NEED TO THINK ABOUT HOW WE **PERFORM** THEM.

YEAH, OKAY... BUT I WANT TO SAY THAT I **DON'T LIKE** TALKING A BUNCH ABOUT FEELINGS LIKE ANGER.

YEAH, ME NEITHER.

OKAY... **THAT** WAS DEEP.

I THINK I NEED A NAP.

"ZZZZZZ"

SEE WHAT WE DID THERE? SWITCHING TO A WORD BALLOON STORY IS A WAY OF STAYING PLAYFUL. IT. BREAKS. THE. PATTERN.

Barking our heads off

Some games have distinct rules, others are far more improvisational. For example, when our family would be having a challenging conversation and perhaps getting stuck on some point or issue, we would sometimes just start barking.

It sounds crazy, but in some contexts it allowed us to express our frustration, vent some emotion, break the pattern of the debate and shift the energy. We understood that the barking was an invitation for all of us to bark, not an act of rejection of the others. It was a moment when we would say, "being in relationships is sometimes difficult so let's get to barking it out!"

Barking is pattern breaking. It reminds us of play. Which reminds us of what we love about each other. Within a few moments, we were often able to return to the conversation and find a path forward. We do it to this day (with or without our son being present). So, WOOF!

- How do playful actions show up during challenging moments?
- Who gets to decide when play is okay during family conflict?
- What is the first step you can take to introduce pattern breaking activities when you feel stuck as a family?

The button game

When our son was just five years old, we took a big sheet of paper and drew buttons, switches and dials all over it. Our whole family decided what the buttons should be called. The labels we created were:

Hug • Mad/Happy • Laugh • Sneeze • Potty • Bark • Sleep • Wake • Sneeze (again) • Fear/Courage, Help Hurt People • Dada, I love you • I'm Hungry, Will you make some food? • Stop Being Grumpy for Daddy • Stop Being Mean

These buttons were about relating. Some buttons addressed very clear interactions required of one specific player (such as "Stop Being Grumpy for Daddy"), while others were purely playful and silly (it's very important to be silly in this game). Others were about expression of emotions.

There were no buttons that said "clean your room" or "do the dishes." These buttons were not about tasks. They were about our way of being. They were invitations for any of us to connect in the moment the button was hit.

The power of this game is its capacity to create significant shifts in how adults and children are choosing to relate. Everyone runs up and hits various buttons, then they fall down and go to sleep, or suddenly frown and get dramatically sad. As we play

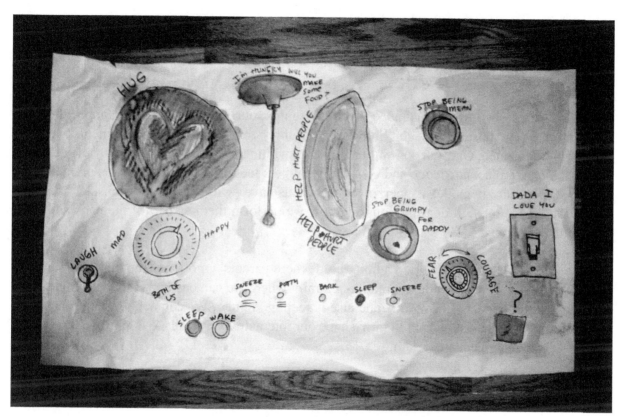

THE BUTTON GAME

the game, we are literally choosing how we want to relate, how we might express our mood and how we want to connect. The dials, which can be turned, move us from mad to happy and back again in mere moments. How we choose to perform those emotions is up to us.

Days later, when Mark was indeed feeling grumpy, our little son ran over and hit the button on the poster that said "Stop Being Grumpy for Daddy." In that moment, two things happened. One, our son was empowered within the safe space created by play to ask his dad to acknowledge and consider what he's feeling. Two, his dad was granted an opportunity to model a superpower each of us have — to consciously consider and if we decide to, shift our emotions and how we perform them as part of the back and forth of relating.

For any of us who grew up in a household where parents' emotions automatically set the tone for the whole house, creating a family where we can easily acknowledge and engage the impact of how someone else is feeling is huge. We can acknowledge that emotions are shaped by, and in turn, shape our interactions. It leads to a family culture of acknowledgment and relating.

What's more, when we make the choice to shift because of the button game — and believe me, when our young child stands with their hand on the button, we can choose to shift — we discover that we really can have some agency over how we are feeling by saying, "We openly acknowledge our emotions *within the relationship.*"

Understanding that emotions are not a state, but a fluid expression that ebbs and flows within relational activities can be hugely empowering. The knowledge that what we feel shapes and, in turn, is shaped in relationship can be liberating.

Thus, having the capacity to shift our emotions within relationship, instead of feeling we are at the mercy of how the world "makes us feel" is a huge lesson the Button Game can help teach us and our children.

And when you make your button poster, *don't forget the hug button. It's awesome!*

- In your family, how do you talk about emotions?
- How might you play with the idea of emotional expression?
- What activities might you play together to "teach" your children how our emotions and relationships are interconnected?

Playing with social rules

Asking our children questions taps their generative potential. Questions invite our children to express their creativity in surprising ways. If you have ever given your children even simple choices, you know what we're talking about.

Parent: Do you want to wear the red shoes or the green shoes for Christmas?
Child: I want to wear both.
Parent: But you can't wear both. You have to choose one.
Child: I choose red and green (as she picks a left red and right green one).

In that moment, we as parents have to ask ourself, are we willing to be playful? Whose rules are we breaking in these moments? What are we creating in letting our child express in these ways? Sometimes, we might allow play to come in and sometimes we might not. There is no one right answer. It depends on the context, our energy level, and the social script (what others will notice or point to). It might be a moment of reframing for the adults.

With younger kids, we typically tend to be more playful, but with older kids, we want them to show us (or others) that they know to play by the rules of what is typically expected of us, especially out in public. What if we, at times, choose to play with the social rules ourselves while our children witness the process?

Openly being a trickster and creating space for both us and our children to explore social expectations can be powerful, leading to conversations about things like resisting peer pressure. It also invites conversations about which social rules we might choose to follow and which ones we might decide to bend. We can talk about how different contexts can impact whether we choose to be playful or not.

What is different when we dance and sing in the park versus in a library? In the morning versus after we are supposed to be in bed? When our children see their parents consciously considering the network of expectations and rules we all inhabit, they come to better understand social contexts are something we collectively construct. We can show our children that we have choices, we have options, and that we have the ability to hold and consider complexity.

When kids are conscious of the ever-shifting context that social expectations are embedded in, they are better able to understand that there are often multiple reasons for why people respond and react in the ways they do.

They also will see that social conformity, peer pressure and other group dynamics can be very destructive if accepted as rules that must always be followed.

- How do you communicate *with* your children about challenging, flexing, and/or breaking social rules?
- How do you engage your uncertainty when you see your child playing with social rules?
- What are the hardest kinds of social rules for you to be playful about? Manners? Public displays of emotion? Why?

ABOUT THAT ANGER THING...

OKAY, REMEMBER BEFORE WHEN WE SAID ANGER CAN BE HIDING *OTHER EMOTIONS?* IT'S A VERY POPULAR WAY OF TALKING ABOUT *ANGER.*

YEAH.

I HAVE A BIT OF A CHALLENGE WITH THAT.

I'M NOT CLEAR ON WHAT IS IMPLIED BY HIDDEN EMOTIONS. THEY'RE HIDDEN INSIDE US?

YEAH, I SEE ... WELL, MAYBE SOME EMOTIONS STAY HIDDEN BECAUSE WE'RE STILL ARRIVING AT THEM?

SURE, THAT'S POSSIBLE, BUT WHAT IF OUR EMOTIONS ARE BEING CREATED, MERGING, AND CHANGING AS PART OF THE PROCESS OF RELATING?

THAT WAY OF THINKING LOCATES OUR EMOTIONS LESS IN THE INDIVIDUAL AND MORE IN THE PROCESS OF RELATING.

YEP. ANOTHER WAY OF THINKING ABOUT IT ...

The caught you doing something right game

Young children may have magnet or sticker boards in their houses to mark the completion of tasks like homework or brushing their teeth. This is a great way of tracking the completion of tasks, but at our house, we took the sticker board a step further, playfully acknowledging that families grow what they focus on, especially when they focus on relationships. Here's how the Caught You Doing Something Right Game works.

A few years back, our six-year-old son would sit at the kitchen table after school, perhaps drawing, and Saliha would enter the room laughing and say, "I caught you!" She might even dance around repeating, "I caught you, I caught you!"

Our son would light up because he knew the game instantly. "What did I do!" he would respond, putting down his pencil.

"What did you catch him doing?" Mark would chime in.

"Guess!" Saliha would demand.

"Give me a clue!" our son would respond.

"Okaaaaaaayyyy," she would say. "It's in the ... bathroom!"

We would all run to the bathroom and jam the doorway, struggling like actors from a silent movie comedy. Our son would finally get in the doorway and stand mystified, scanning our small bathroom. Finally he would say, "I don't know? What did I do! Tell me!!!"

Saliha would extend her hand and point dramatically at the towel rack where his towel was hung up. "I hung up my towel," he would holler.

"Yep, and that means you get a sticker," Saliha responded racing out the door back towards the living room where we had hung up a poster board. There on the board was not just his name but columns with our names as well, stickers trailing off beneath each.

Saliha would take a sticker and add it to our son's column. Then she would examine the board. "Hmmm," she said, "Dad's not getting very many stickers. Is that because he's not doing anything good?"

"Oh well," Mark would say, wandering back towards his work.

"I caught you, Daddy!" our son would holler.

Mark would spin around. "What did I do?"

"You are making dinner!" he replied, and so he was. Which resulted in a sticker for Mark.

For a time, we had an agreement that fifty stickers equaled a bowl of ice cream. Later that became an app. Stickers could be awarded for a wide range of actions, and as time passed, those included more nuanced actions like noticing or supporting, choices that showed caring and kindness.

So, not only did we note when a towel was hung up, we noted when a person's point of view was acknowledged, when someone came back and made something right, when a person showed compassion or empathy. "Hey, I saw what you did there!" we would call out. Or "I saw that!" And so, we gave witness to what otherwise might have passed by without being marked.

We had an agreement that no one can give themselves a sticker or call out their own good actions. (Some hinting crept in. This was part of the play.) Negotiating the agreements and designing changes are a huge part of the game, allowing it to evolve as our children grow older. In playing in these ways, we practiced more important relational capacities: negotiation, flexibility, and agreement. The rewards can be anything, the limits and rules can be whatever they need to be. But the dynamic it creates is threefold.

First, the game invites our children to try and figure out what they did right. In the moment of trying to guess, they become very receptive to the answer. Because of this, the value of actions like successfully hanging up their towel is heightened for them. This may lead to a repeat of good behavior that contributes to the orderly operation of the household. Better yet, once an action is repeated a few times, it can become habit. This can be about towels or it can be about empathy. This is one of the long-term-goals of the Caught You Doing Something Right Game. We modify behavior by highlighting what is going well instead of only highlighting mistakes.

Second, the game creates an opportunity for hilarious play; an outburst of playful energy for families. In a world where we can often get bogged down in the tasks, lists, and demands of daily life, it reminds us of how fun family life can be. We are also reminded that playfully noticing and acknowledging the efforts of others is huge fun, and fun is the glue that keeps communication flowing. The intention to create this space of relational joy is the real lesson of the game. It may seem to be about marking and acknowledging good behavior, but it's actually about intentionally relating in joyful ways.

Finally, the game shifts our focus as parents to creating and appreciating a relational family culture. In the midst of a busy life, it reminds us to focus on and celebrate what happens in the back and forth between human beings. It is no accident that parents get stickers, too. Our children are told to say thank you but when a child catches a parent "doing something right" they are learning a crucial relational lesson — that we are all contributing and that we all need support and acknowledgment.

Oh, and wait until you get a sticker from your partner when your child is not even around. *Trust me, it's magic.*

- How often do you notice what is working well versus what is not working well in your family life?
- How do you appreciate each other for the relational acts (offers of care and connection) within your family?
- What playful activities might you design that are inclusive of all family members being noticed for their relational contributions?

The don't let 'em off the bed game

As parents, we hold our babies close and teach them to associate our warmth, voices and touch with their own security. Then, one day, as they grow older we may find ourselves shying away from offering that comfort. Why?

We shouldn't shy away from physical touch with our children just because they're gangling nine-year-olds playing baseball, and yet the impulse is there. Our culture's prohibitions against touch parallel those that tell our sons to hide their emotional expression. It's all part of the drumbeat message that boys need to toughen up.

Since touch is associated with comforting little children, our sons may feel the need to prove they are no longer little kids by shying away from our comforting gestures. We, in turn, may want to avoid hugging or holding hands in public, so as not to embarrass our sons or daughters. These social pressures to disconnect both emotionally and physically from our children are real. And they are woefully misguided. But our children cannot be the ones to challenge the unspoken prohibitions against loving, caring contact. It has to be us.

One great way to bridge that challenging set of ideas, and keep physical connection normalized, is to wrestle. Our favorite wrestling game was the Don't Let 'Em Off the Bed Game.

Sometimes, the three of us would be lying on the bed reading or talking and suddenly the wrestling game would just start up. The goal of the game was to get free and step away from the bed. Whomever did that was the winner. This made a hilarious dynamic by which two people would struggle to keep one person from getting loose, and then suddenly another would start to get untangled and they would get teamed up on. Finally, someone would jump to their feet and step back, cheering.

Wrestling can help us bridge to more comforting forms of contact, such as holding hands or cuddling because wrestling continues to normalize touch and increase the frequency of connection as our kids as they grow up. Its important to maintain more calming forms of touch with our kids as well. We can keep the connection of touch going, all we have to do is make the conscious choice not to stop.

As part of growing relational intelligence, we need to show our children the ways humans connect through platonic, non-sexualized touch. Only through years of connection and touch can our sons and daughters truly gain confidence in their own healthy ways of making physical contact. In this way, we contribute to a culture of mutual respect, consent, and safety.

Our children need the solid baseline of love and connection our touch gives them. It is one more powerful space from which they can launch themselves into the world. Don't stop holding hands, leaning on each other on the train or reading your children a book and holding them close as they fall off to sleep. It will reinforce for them that they are loved, beyond all the words that we will ever speak.

- When do you typically embrace your child?
- What were your favorite moments of contact with your child? Do they still occur?
- Does physical contact increase or decrease during times when you disagree with your children? With your partner? Why?
- What is the history of touch in your family of origin?

Be patient toward all that is unsolved in your heart and try to love the questions themselves ...

And the point is, to live everything.
Live the questions now. Perhaps you will then gradually, without noticing it, live along some distant day into the answer.

Rainer Maria Rilke

Part thirteen:

The sadness ghost

Play amidst crisis

The following story recounts how powerful a force play can be during a time of emotional challenge. It is not a happy story. It has no sandboxes or birthday cakes. It does not echo with the laughter of children. In fact, it is infused with grief, fear, and deep loss. But it is a story about powerful forms of play nonetheless.

If we restrict play to the land of happy emotions, we lose our understanding of its wider purpose. Play is about ideas and how we hold them, move them, shift them and find ways to live through, around, and past the destructive impact they can sometimes have.

Mark originally wrote this story in 2012. It appeared in *Psychotherapy Networker* magazine.

Sadness
ghost ↑

The Sadness Ghost
A six-year-old's drawing
of his own sadness

The Sadness Ghost

In the summer of 2011, an eight-year-old boy was murdered here in New York City. He got lost walking the few blocks home from day camp. It's a chilling story, even more so for parents of young children.

When I first read about it, my response was, "I have to get my son away from the city. This place isn't safe. We have to go somewhere safe." Close on the heels of that thought came the question of how to get my son — who's six, sweet, full of energy, and talkative — not to trust strangers. What if some guy takes my boy away? Even as I write this, I'm feeling the grief of possible loss.

A few days later my son looked down at a newspaper lying on the sidewalk. It read, "Missing Brooklyn Boy Found Murdered" and had a picture of the boy staring up at us. My son, who can read, asked me what it meant. I haltingly explained that someone the boy didn't know killed him. I used simple language and moved through the explanation quickly and in a neutral tone, but I didn't lie. I told him that, sometimes, strangers could be dangerous.

In a quiet voice, he said, "This is bad." And we walked on toward the park.

To this day, I don't know whether it was the right decision, to be honest with him while we stood there, looking down at that newspaper. I felt the weight of the world settle on my six-year-old son and me. It was one of those moments when simplified stories or outright lies seem like a much better idea.

A few nights later, I found out he had been crying at his mother's house (we are no longer married) and that he was sad because of a song on the radio that he'd heard months before at my home. The song was "American Pie" by Don McLean. You probably know the lyrics:

"Bye, bye Miss American Pie / Drove my Chevy to the levee, but the levee was dry / Them good ol' boys were drinking whiskey and rye, singing / This'll be the day that I die / This'll be the day that I die."

"He's has been crying all evening," his mother told me. "He doesn't want to hear 'American Pie' anymore," she said. I realized then that his simple response, "This is bad," had only been the tip of the iceberg.

A day or so later, my son was talking with his stepmother, Saliha and me. He told her he was very sad. "I've been sad for three days, and I don't want to be sad anymore."

Saliha, who is a couple and family therapist, asked him what was making him sad. He told us he was thinking about death. He then put his hands over his ears, lay down on his side, and shut his eyes. He cried about Olive, our cat that had died a couple of years before. I thought, "I shouldn't have told him about the boy." I felt a chill in my gut — the feeling that I'd done something irreversible.

Saliha asked him about his sadness. He said he just couldn't stop feeling sad. He has a little tray full of plastic figures he's been collecting called Toonz. He has about 40 of them. He looked at us and said, "What's the point of collecting things if I'm going to die? What will happen to them when I'm dead?" He repeated that he didn't want to be sad anymore and that he couldn't stop thinking about it.

Saliha said, "Close your eyes and picture something for me. I want you to think about an orange. Can you picture it?"

He said, "Yes."

Saliha said, "OK, now I want you to stop thinking about it."

Our sweet son opened his eyes and looked at Saliha. He closed his eyes again. "OK," he said.

"Stop thinking about how the orange peel smells. Stop thinking about how the orange tastes. Don't think about how the peel looks when you tear part of it off."

"I can't stop thinking about it because you keep talking about it!" he yelled, equal parts exasperated and amused.

"OK," said Saliha. "Now think about an apple."

"OK," he said.

"Think about its red color," said Saliha.

"Green," he said. "I like green apples."

"OK," said Saliha, "think about its green color. Think about how it tastes. Think about how crunchy and tart it is. Now," said Saliha. "can you see the orange?"

"No," he said, amused.

"If you want to stop thinking about something, you can't just tell yourself to stop. You have to think about something else," she said. "You grow what you focus on. So if you think about sadness, you'll grow sadness. If you think about happiness, you'll grow that. Think of the orange as sadness and the apple as happiness. If you want to stop thinking about the orange, you have to think about something else, about the happiness, about the apple."

My son took the oranges and apples idea and, within a few moments, he'd reassigned ice cream as the happiness thought. We talked about what would be examples of "ice cream thoughts." We talked more about choosing what thoughts we might want to grow so as not to feel sad. Bedtime came, I read him some books, and he went to sleep.

Later, Saliha posed the following question: "Why is sadness necessarily a bad thing? We can hold sadness just like other emotions. It's part of life. Sadness can even be good. It's how we relate to it."

The next morning, my son woke and called to me that he'd had a bad dream. "I dreamed that Mommy went away for two years," he told me. I got him out of his bed and we began our day. We sat at the dining table, which, as usual, was covered in our art supplies. He said Mommy was gone, and it made him sad. I asked him to tell me more about the dream. We talked about sadness and he returned to the subject of his toys and death. He said he didn't want to collect any more toys. What was the use? (A hell of a good existential question, by the way.)

Then something magical happened. It's been a while since that day, and I'm sure I'm not constructing it entirely accurately, but I recently found a page in a journal that I'd flipped open that morning and made notes as my son was speaking to me.

He and I are both artists. We draw pictures. We often draw them as a way to order our thoughts about the world, or to construct stories that help us experience it. As we spoke, I asked him again about sadness — not death, but sadness. Saliha's concern that we not try to hide from sadness was on my mind. And then one of us, I don't know which, said, "What if sadness is a cartoon? How would we draw it? How would sadness look?"

My son got his pencils and he drew the Sadness Ghost. The drawing he did that morning is reproduced at the beginning of this story. He was very specific. He drew the eyes several times. I had a second sheet of paper, on which I drew versions of the ghost with different eyes, and he said, "No, Daddy, those aren't right."

The eyes he drew were blank and ghostly, but they're not angry or mean. My son can draw angry and mean eyes. He draws them all the time on his dragons. These eyes were lost, and perhaps worried. But they were also, as he described them, "cute."
In the moment he conceptualized the Sadness Ghost, he activated his own solution for processing what he was feeling. In that moment, he ceased to be a sad person and became, instead, a person who was being visited by sadness. This distinction is crucial in processing powerful, sometimes-overwhelming emotions like rage, fear, or grief.

Together, we created our story for the Sadness Ghost. We talked about being "visited by sadness." We talked about how sadness wasn't always a bad thing; that we all feel sad sometimes.

Then he said, "The Sadness Ghost comes and goes. It's OK for the Sadness Ghost to come. He can come for a little while because he's cute. He comes to me as a hiding place for him because he's scared. But later, he has to go when he's not too scared."

This little boy then played the role of himself speaking to the Sadness Ghost. "OK, now go," he said gently, gesturing for the ghost to go, indicating that we each have to know when to tell sadness to move on. What's remarkable is how he was able to

207

accept sadness into himself in the form of the Sadness Ghost, *and then care for it*.

He became the caretaker of his own sadness; he became the safe place where his sadness could come to be comforted. He no longer defined himself as sad. He was being visited by sadness — a very different way to frame the experience.

In the days after that, our son's sadness went away. He went back to collecting things with a vengeance. He moved on to his ice-cream thoughts, and although sadness will visit him many times in his life, I hope his capacity to hold it will remain as vital and powerful as it was that morning.

Part fourteen:

Relating is life

In the beautiful back and forth

For us, *The Relational Book for Parenting* represents the hub of a vast wheel of ideas; a hub that links enough different ways of looking at relationships that most of us can find a familiar entry point. And in that moment, we all can feel welcome in the conversation. Which brings us to the core message of our book: in the back and forth of relating, we remake the world.

In 2010, AARP conducted a survey that revealed a startling conclusion. One in three American adults aged forty-five or older is "chronically lonely." That's 42 million Americans, up from one in five, only ten years before. What's worse, studies show that loneliness is equal to smoking a pack a day in terms of increased risk for mortality.

Judith Shulevitz, writing for *The New Republic*, reports in her article titled "The Lethality of Loneliness":

"A partial list of the physical diseases thought to be caused by or exacerbated by loneliness would include Alzheimer's, obesity, diabetes, high blood pressure, heart disease, neurodegenerative diseases, and even cancer — tumors can metastasize faster in lonely people."

Where does all this loneliness come from? Human beings need decades to do the trial and error work of growing our relational capacities. Instead, our culture blocks us from doing this work. In turn, we tell our young sons to "man up." We tell our young daughters that only certain emotions are appropriate, driving darker, more challenging feelings underground to devastating effect. The result of our culture of relational suppression is a uniquely American epidemic of loneliness.

When our children are blocked from growing their relational capacities, it negatively impacts more than just their longevity. It negatively impacts every personal and professional metric by which we measure quality of life over the course of their lifetimes. Sadly, it will also negatively impact the lives of those around them and those who come after.

The word authentic comes up several times in this book. Our particular use of the word comes out of spaces where our sons and daughters are forced to hide the distinctive parts of themselves in order to fit our culture's rules for being a "real man" or a "real woman." For us, being authentic is an action we can take as we relate to others. It is in relating that we can choose to share what makes us distictive. Relational intelligence includes, as part of its core benefits, ways in which we can share, hold, and value difference. When our children learn to express what makes them distinctive, they also learn to value that expression in others.

Relational intelligence isn't just about keeping our relationships running more smoothly. Relational intelligence fuels connection, collaboration and innovation — exactly the skills employers say they will need in the coming decades. In a more relational world, the expression of what makes each of us distinctive will give value to our partners, co-workers, and communities.

We have the power to ensure that the damaging aspects of our culture do not suppress the natural relational gifts our children are born with. As parents, we can model for our children what it means to center our relationships and grow connection in the world. We can give them a space in which to grow their relationship superpowers, and in doing so, create the promise of community for generations to come, designing a new culture of connection in a world starving for it.

We simply have to choose to do so.

In closing, we'd like to invite you to stay in touch. You can now be part of this larger conversation, so reach out with questions or ideas. If you would like to join us for workshops, please do so. With everyone's help, online and elsewhere, in every space where we come together to connect and share ideas, we can collectively grow our relational capacities.

So, come play!

Saliha Bava and Mark Greene
ThinkPlayPartners.com

Part fifteen:

More to read and watch

More resources on relating

- Anderson, H. (1997). *Conversation, language and possibility*. Basic.

- Bateson, P. & Martin, P. (2013). *Play, playfulness, creativity and innovation*. Cambridge University Press.

- Chu, J. (2014). *When boys become boys: Development, relationships, and masculinity.* NYU Press.

- Cohen, L. (2002). *Playful parenting: An exciting new approach to raising children that will help you nurture close connections, solve behavior problems, and encourage confidence.* Ballantine Books.

- Gergen, K. (2009). *Relational being: Beyond self and community.* Oxford University Press.

- Kelley, T. & Kelley, D. (2013). *Creative confidence: Unleashing the creative potential within us all.* The Crown Publishing Group.

- McNamee, S. & Moscheta, M. (2015) *Relational intelligence and collaborative learning*. In: New Directions in Teaching & Learning. Vol. 143. pp. 25-40. Wiley

- Pearce, B. (2007). *Making social worlds: A communication perspective.* Blackwell Publishing.

- Pink, D. (2006). *A whole new mind: Why right-brainers will rule the future.* Penguin.

- Raser, J. (1999). *Raising children you can live with*. Bayou Publishing.

- Salit, C. (2016). *Performance breakthrough. A radical approach to success at work.* Hachette Books.

- Siegel, D. & Bryson, T. P. (2012). *The whole-brain child: 12 revolutionary strategies to nurture your child's developing mind.* Bantam.

- Schwarz, R. & Braff, E. (2011). *We're no fun anymore.* Routledge.

- Sutton-Smith, B. (1997). *The ambiguity of play.* Harvard University Press.

- Tegano, D. (1990). *Relationship of tolerance of ambiguity and playfulness to creativity.* Psychological Reports 66, pp. 1047-1056.

- Thomas, D. & Seely Brown, J. (2011). *A new culture of learning: Cultivating the imagination for a world of constant change.* CreateSpace.

- Way, N. (2011). *Deep secrets.* Harvard University Press.

View TED Talks (TED talks retrieved from https://www.ted.com):

- Chimamanda Adichie: *The danger of a single story*

- Lisa Feldman Barrett: *You aren't at the mercy of your emotions*

- Stuart Brown: *Play is more than just fun*

- Nicholas Christakis: *The hidden influence of social networks*

- Mihaly Csikszentmihalyi: *Flow, the secret to happiness*

- Anne Curzan: *What makes a word real*

- John Koenig: *Beautiful new words to describe obscure emotions*

- Ken Robinson: *Do schools kill creativity*

- Tiffany Watt Smith: *The history of human emotions*

- Adora Svitak: *What adults can learn from kids*

- Gabe Zichermann: *How games make kids smarter*

Saliha's thank you

I dedicate this book to my parents who practiced the art of growing as parents alongside their children. I also dedicate this book to two teachers: Prof. R.K. Hebsur, at Tata Institute of Social Sciences, who introduced me to philosophy of social sciences; and to Prof. Jim Keller at Virginia Tech, who introduced me to Harlene Anderson, Ken Gergen, Harry Goolishian, Sheila McNamee, John Shotter, and Michael White's writings, which put me on the path of my own life's work.

Thank you Mercy College for funding my play scholarship. Thanks to my HGI and Taos Institute communities of practice. To my students, supervisees, and clients who trusted the process, took risks, and opened up, allowing me to play along as you reinvented yourselves — thank you! You all taught me to trust the creative process that is this book.

Thank you to my sisters, brother-in-law, and nieces for supporting my creative ventures. To Gus, whose playful trickster spirit grounded me in the ideas of performance and play, the waters I was swimming in when I met you. And to Mark, my co-author, playmate, anchor, and co-designer, without whom I wouldn't have arrived at this book. Thank you all for being you! I learn along with you everyday. As Green Day sings:

"It's something unpredictable, but in the end it's right. I hope you have the time of your life."

- Saliha

Mark Greene — @RemakingManhood

Founder of Remaking Manhood, Author, Filmmaker, Activist, Dad
Mark's articles on the suppression of boys' emotional expression, parenting, men's issues and culture have been shared over 250,000 times on social media, resulting in over 20 million page views. He has written and spoken about men's issues at *The Good Men Project*, *Salon*, *Shriver Report*, *Uplift Connect*, *Yes! Magazine*, *BBC* and the *New York Times*. Mark is also an Emmy-winning animator and cartoonist. Mark's book, *Remaking Manhood* is available at RemakingManhood.com

Saliha Bava, Ph.D. — @ThinkPlay

Couple and Family Therapist, Researcher, and Professor, Author, Mom
Saliha is a couple and family therapist, a consultant, and researcher in New York City. She is an Associate Professor of Marriage and Family Therapy at Mercy College, N.Y. She serves on the board of International Certificate in Collaborative-Dialogic Practices, on the advisory board of Taos Institute, and served on the board (2012-2017) of American Family Therapy Academy. For 20-plus years, she has consulted, designed and implemented play-based and dialogic change processes with organizational, community, family, learning, and research systems. She focuses on how adults play, hyperlinked identity, trauma, community, coupling, leading, and collaboration. Visit SalihaBava.com to learn about her practice and http://thinkplaypartners.com/playlab for her research.

Picture books to grow kids' relational capacities from ThinkPlayPartners.com

The Naughty Hand — This is the full-color story of Milo, an energetic and excitable six-year-old who can't stop grabbing and pushing other kids. One day, he pushes his friend Owen too hard and causes a scraped knee.

With the help of some very unusual friends (designed by the book's six-year-old co-author) Milo goes on to solve his problem.

The Naughty Hand is designed to help younger children reflect on their own and other's choices, **helping to create more self-aware interactions.**

Flatmunder — When the little girl across the street tells Bernard there are flat witches in his bathroom, Bernard begins to worry ... a lot. Then, one night, Bernard meets a new friend called Flatmunder and a whole house full of flat witches. Together they help Bernard come to terms with his fears and discover that when we change the way we think about things, they change too. **A full-color story about kids' fears and the power of play.**

Who do you know that would LOVE this book?

1. Share *The Relational Book for Parenting* with others in your parenting networks or family! Put a copy in their hands!

2. Tell others about our book on social media. Rate us on Amazon! Hashtag: #RelationalBook and @ThinkPlayPrtnrs (Note: p-r-t-n-r-s)

3. Watch our videos and join our online workshops at ThinkPlayPartners.com

Thanks for sharing relational thinking to make a better world! — Mark and Saliha

Think Play Partners nyc

Made in the USA
Middletown, DE
20 February 2022